MARY MASHUTA'S

Confetti QUILTS

A NO-FUSS APPROACH TO COLOR, FABRIC & DESIGN

To Colleen —
Fabric & color —
too much is not enough
Mary Mashuta 11-04

C&T PUBLISHING

DEDICATION

Quiltmaking teachers, like rock stars, have their "groupies." These are the loyal folks who sign up for the teacher's classes again and again. I dedicate this book to my groupies. They learn from me and I learn an equal amount from them. It has been truly wonderful to see them grow as quiltmakers over the years.

© 2003 Mary Mashuta

Editor-in-Chief: Darra Williamson

Editor: Liz Aneloski

Technical Editor: Carolyn Aune

Second Technical Editor: Katrina Lamken

Copyeditor: Stacy Chamness

Proofreader: Stacy Chamness

Cover Designer: Christina Jarumay

Design Director/Book Designer: Rose Sheifer

Illustrator: Tim Manibusan

Production Assistant: Jeff Carrillo

Digital Photography: Diane Pedersen

Quilt Photography: Sharon Risedorph

Published by C&T Publishing, Inc., P.O. Box 1456, Lafayette, California 94549

Front cover: A Few Days in Provence, Mary Mashuta

Back cover: Kailua-Kona Escape, Becky Keck and *Triad Stars*, Mary Mashuta

Library of Congress Cataloging-in-Publication Data

Mashuta, Mary.
    Mary Mashuta's confetti quilts : a no-fuss approach to color, fabric & design.
        p. cm.
    ISBN 1-57120-195-5 (paper trade)
    1. Patchwork--Patterns. 2. Quilting--Patterns. I. Title.
    TT835 .M27368 2003
    746.46'041--dc21

                                        2002151473

Printed in China

CONTENTS

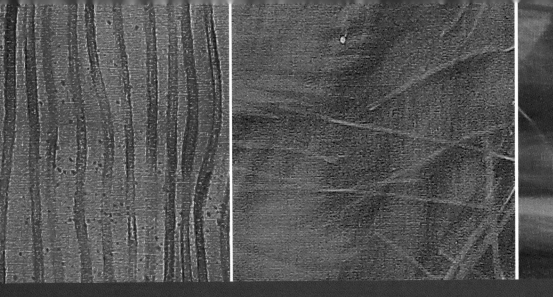

INTRODUCTION

All quilters buy colored fabric! I have taught color classes for years, but what I really teach is how to select colored fabric (the more the better) and make quilts with it. Where you place which fabric is design, another intimidating word. But every time you make a quilt you make design decisions, deciding which colored fabric to put where. In this book, I try to present the information in a simple and straight forward way.

I list design rules for each quilt because they all have rules. There are also design hints—tasty tidbits for you to munch on while you "read" the pictures. These hints are like candy or chips—who can eat only one? If you like words also, they are here for you to read about your favorite quilts.

Many quilters want instant projects and fast results, but others are willing to invest a little more time to get things "right." It's frustrating,

however, if you can't figure out what "right" is. One of the wonderful things about making quilts is there is no one right answer. I've picked six blocks and a half dozen or so "right answer" quilts for each block, but many more are possible. You'll even be able to come up with a "right answer" using your own fabrics and colors. The blocks are fairly simple to cut and stitch, so you can concentrate on fabric and color choices rather than complicated construction. The project quilts with directions in the back of the book will help you get started.

I encourage you to try a new fabric style, color, or color scheme you haven't used before. Most of the quilts presented in this book came from classes I taught. The makers had to work with specific rules, color schemes, or styles of fabric as part of their class assignment. They all stretched to try new things, and were surprised and

pleased with the results.

You may already have discovered that the process becomes as important as the product for many of us. I recommend you use some kind of design wall to "park" your fabric pieces on while you compose your quilt. Then you can study and think about your quilt, rather than just finishing it as quickly as possible. If you don't have a design wall, I include information on how to make one.

I have discovered that by increasing the number of fabrics and colors you use you can turn simple blocks into exciting blocks, and exciting blocks into exciting quilts. I really believe that as far as fabric and color are concerned, "too much is not enough." So, find a comfortable chair, curl up, and let's get started because, believe it or not, exciting quilts don't have to be complicated.

CHAPTER ONE

What's All the Fuss About Color?

Many wonderful quilts have been made by quilters who never officially studied color. If you are unsure of your color choices, learning a little about color theory can help you to be more confident in picking colors to use together. I will discuss some standard color schemes and show you how I made up some new schemes after learning how colors relate to each other.

Picking colors for your house or quilt can be fun. Photo by author.

ARRANGING COLORS

There are several ways of arranging colors so you can see how they relate to one another.

Color Band

A color band places the colors in a logical progression or flow. (Children can do the same thing with a box of crayons!) There can be infinite steps along the band. Color bands are rainbows made of colored paper. Here is the one my sister and I made in college with little ⅜ inch strips of paper that were painted with paint we mixed ourselves. It's not perfect, but we sure learned a lot.

Color Band made by Mary Mashuta and Roberta Horton. 1960s.

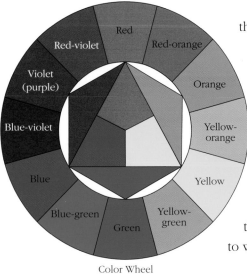

Color Wheel

Red, yellow, and blue are the three primary colors and are found in the center of this particular color wheel. The other colors on the color wheel are created by combining the primary colors.

Blending two primary colors creates a secondary color. Red and yellow make the secondary color orange. Yellow and blue make the secondary color green. And, blue and red make the secondary color violet. (We usually call it purple.)

The tertiary colors are the two-name colors; red-orange, yellow-orange and so on.

You can refer to a wheel to figure out the basic color schemes, or ways of combining colors. Color wheels are merely tools, not the gospel. The actual colors vary from printing to printing and wheel to wheel.

As a quilter, I might look at a color wheel to come up with a new set of colors to try or find an accent color to spark my quilt. Many of the people who made quilts for this book got out their color wheels as a first step to choose colors for their quilts. The color wheel is just a tool. Play with it.

BASIC COLOR SCHEMES

MONOCHROMATIC means using just one color plus its tints (the color plus white), shades (the color plus black), and tones (the color plus gray). The family who painted the house below realized that tints and shades of beige would be much more interesting than just using beige by itself.

Color Wheel

A color wheel is another way of arranging colors in a logical progression. It is a circle—no beginning and no end. Basically, a color wheel illustrates how colors relate to each other.

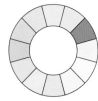

Monochromatic

Tints and shades of one color make a monochromatic color scheme. Berkeley, California. Photo by author.

ANALOGOUS colors are next to each other on the color wheel. They are related like family members. They are different, but share some common traits. Analogous schemes are the easiest to create because they share common colors.

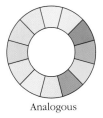
Analogous

Orange, yellow, and yellow-green are an analogous color scheme. Pacific Grove, California. Photo by author.

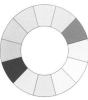
Complementary

COMPLEMENTARY colors are opposite each other on the color wheel. They bring out the truest color in each other. Christmas red and green are complements, but so are blue and orange, and blue-green and red-orange. Each hue (color) has its complement (the color across from it on the color wheel).

SPLIT COMPLEMENTS begin with the complementary colors. If we begin with blue and orange, we eliminate orange and substitute red-orange and yellow-orange, which are the colors on each side of orange. Or, we can eliminate blue and substitute blue-violet and blue-green. We can also eliminate our two starting colors and get DOUBLE SPLIT COMPLEMENTS.

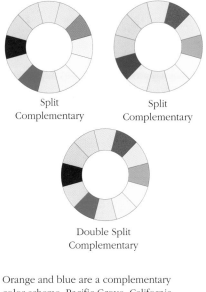

Split Complementary

Split Complementary

Double Split Complementary

Orange and blue are a complementary color scheme. Pacific Grove, California. Photo by author.

Making up a new scheme. Is this an analogous complementary color scheme? Berkeley, California. Photo by author.

Creating New Complementary Schemes

Sometimes we can make up new schemes. This building is painted yellow/yellow-green and violet/red-violet. Two colors next to each other are paired with their complementary partners across the wheel. Would you call these ANALOGOUS COMPLEMENTS?

Analogous
Complementary

I made up another color scheme that goes a step further. I call it EXTENDED COMPLEMENTARY. You pick two complementary colors, and add the colors on both sides of the complements. In this way, the scheme is not so obvious. I have yet to find a building painted in extended complements, but you will be able to enjoy quilts in this book using the scheme.

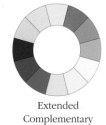

Extended
Complementary

TRIAD color schemes are made up of three colors equally spaced around the color wheel. Not too many people paint their houses using this scheme, but I did find this building.

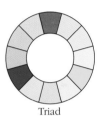

Triad

The primary colors of red, yellow, and blue are a triad color scheme. Berkeley, California. Photo by author.

A POLYCHROMATIC color scheme is another basic scheme. It uses all the colors around the color wheel. The colors don't all have to be the full saturated colors. They can be muted (grayed) or tinted (lightened).

Polychromatic

Polychromatic color schemes don't have to look like rainbows. Berkeley, California. Photo by author.

This subtle polychromatic scheme uses all the colors. Miami, Florida. Photo by Roberta Horton.

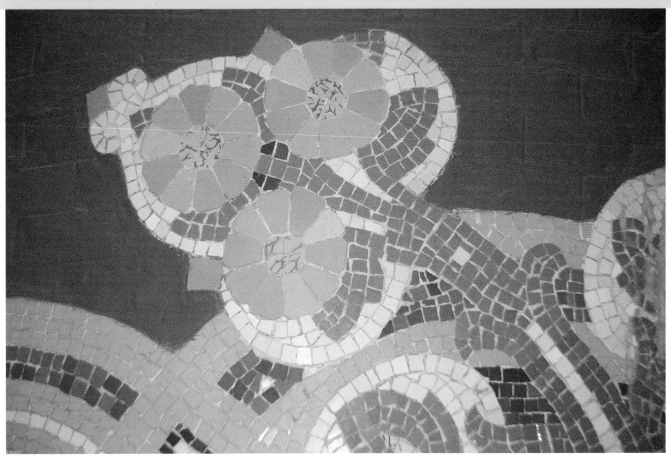

Within each color selected, strive for slight differences. Barcelona, Spain. Photo by Roberta Horton.

OVER-MATCHING

Choosing a color scheme is just a beginning. When you pick your fabrics, try to find many fabrics that are just slightly different from each other in color—some lighter, some darker, some warmer, some cooler, some duller, some brighter. Over-matching makes for a lifeless quilt; slight differences in color make a quilt more lively.

Putting the fabrics together to make a quilt is different than picking the clothes you wear everyday; you may work hard to make the colors of your clothes match each other exactly. When you pick your quilting fabrics, try to find many versions of the colors in your color scheme.

Quilters who have studied art learn to use warm and cool versions of their colors at the same time. (For example, a red may be slightly warmer than your beginning red fabric because it was mixed with a little more yellow. Or, it might be a little cooler because it has just a tad more blue in it.) Even if I'm using hand-dyed gradations or a set of coordinated fabrics designed as a collection where the colors are perfectly matched, I like to add in some more fabric that isn't "matchy-matchy."

Also, remember that lighter and darker versions of your colors add value contrast; duller and brighter versions add variety of intensity. One of the reasons old scrap quilts made from what was around are so lively is because the fabrics couldn't be coordinated and made to match.

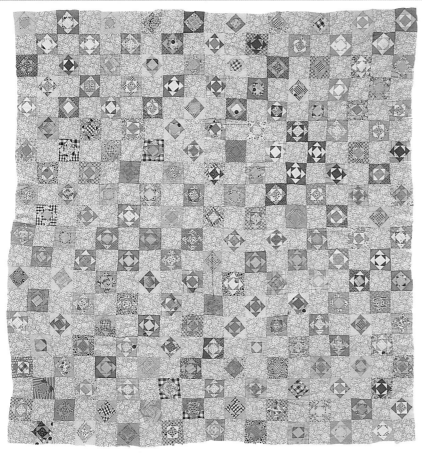

The quilter made-do when she ran out of fabric while piecing a block.

Square within a Square. 76" x 80" top, mid-twentieth century. Collection of the author. Hand pieced blocks joined with machine stitching.

SCRAP QUILTS

Polychromatic

Many 30s-era quilts just happen to be polychromatic because they were made from available scraps. Quilters had to make-do. West Virginia quilters referred to their quilts as being "blended." When a quilt was blended, it was right.

Modern quilters can learn a lot by making a true scrap quilt with "real" scraps, not just fat quarters from the quilt store. Then you really have to make-do with what's on hand. Susan Dague has a large collection of feed sack and other vintage fabrics because she started buying and using them in the 1980s. She made this scrap quilt to try and reduce her pile of scraps, but barely made a dent in it!

Sixteen-Patch Pinwheel. 59" x 71". 2002. Susan Dague, Piedmont, California. Made from feed sack and other vintage fabric scraps.

Amtrak-Am-Slow. 1982. Mary Mashuta.

Pushed-Neutrals

In the early 1980s, before gradations of hand-dyed fabrics were available to quilters, I wished for them. One day I visited local quilt stores and purchased all the solid grays and beiges I could find, becoming frustrated because they weren't a perfect gradation. Nonetheless, I pieced a vest using thirteen of the fabrics.

The result, *Amtrak-Am-Slow*, turned out much better than I had thought it would. I discovered that the slight mismatching worked better because it wasn't so perfect. The PUSHED-NEUTRAL color scheme was born. I taught quilters how to make pushed-neutral vests for years. Students enjoyed learning to pick their own colors because there was no one right answer.

Pushed-neutrals are all about mismatching. You pick a color on the color wheel and then find four slightly different medium to medium-light versions of it—some a little warmer, some a little cooler.

The four colors are then paired with four neutrals; either three beiges and one gray or three grays and one beige. Again, you want some warmer and some cooler. The one different neutral is thrown in to liven things up.

On page 13 are some pushed-neutral color schemes.

Pushed-neutrals taught my students and me about the beauty of mis-matching. When hand-dyed gradations did become available, it only took one project for me to realize how boring perfectly matched colors could be. If you have some hand-dyed gradations in your stash, spark them up by mixing them with some commercial solids. They will be a different color temperature, adding interest to your collection.

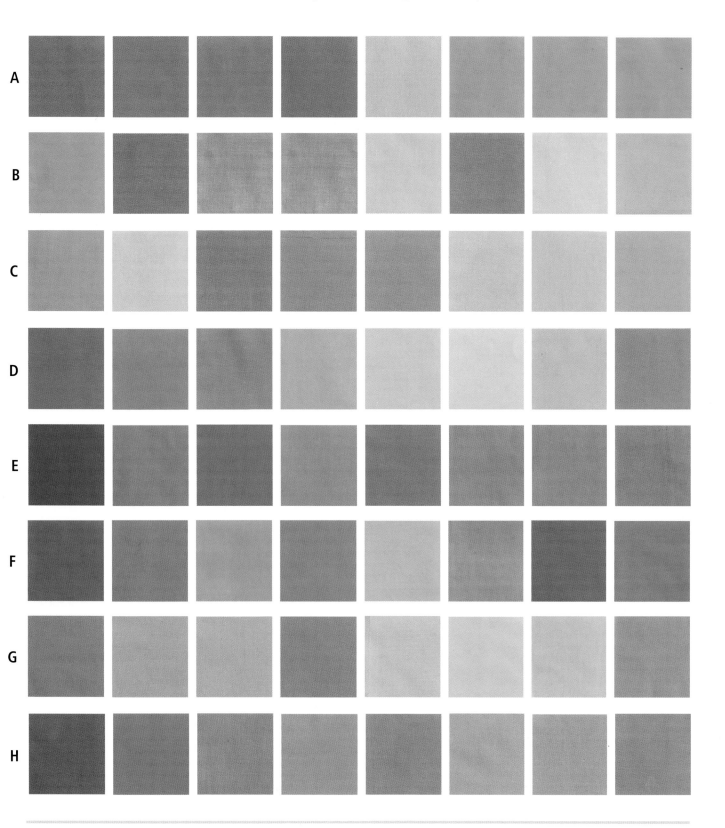

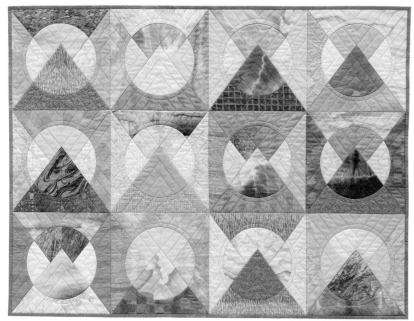

Atmospheres. 48" x 36". 1998. Rebecca Rohrkaste, Berkeley, California. In the collection of Diana McClun. Moon over the Mountain block.

Gay Nichols was not an art major in college, but she has studied color by taking art and quilt classes since she became a quilter. She views art exhibitions, really looks at what she sees in nature, and learns by doing as she paints and makes quilts. As the sun sinks behind the Golden Gate Bridge, Gay sees reflected sunsets on a hill outside her windows. She combines her knowledge of color and art with what she sees to create her quilts.

An 1840 four-patch quilt in a quilt calendar provided a starting place for Gay. She likes to combine what she sees in nature with traditional quilt patterns.

Polychromatic

ARTFUL QUILTS

Many advanced quilters don't worry about all this color stuff. Look at the following two beautiful quilts made by accomplished quilters who have studied color but now work intuitively and don't worry about color wheels. Both began with traditional blocks.

Rebecca Rohrkaste, who went to the Rhode Island School of Design, is known as an accomplished colorist. She "does subtle" beautifully. She has done a whole series of Moon over the Mountain quilts. It's not necessary to reinvent the wheel every time you make a quilt. Once you understand how a block works, you can concentrate on your color and fabric choices.

Reflected Sunset. 64" x 76". 2002. Gay Nichols, Albany, California. Based on 1880 four-patch quilt.

LEARNING MORE ABOUT COLOR

I learn about color by looking and seeing what's around me. If you want to become more aware, you can use a color wheel to help you analyze what you are looking at. (Small, inconspicuous ones are available.)

Get up from where you are sitting now and go into the kitchen. Open the cupboard where you store canned goods and analyze the container labels. My oatmeal comes in a box with a triad color scheme, my tomatoes come in a can with a complementary scheme.

Go around your house and make a color scheme list. I tallied paintings, needlework, large and small quilts, area rugs, and carpets. I was surprised how many polychromatic items I had. If you need more practice, visit open homes for sale, model homes, and decorator show houses. (The first two are free and provide good Sunday afternoon entertainment.)

Check out the quilts in your local quilt show or at a national venue. Get past simply looking at your favorite schemes.

Visit an art exhibit or look at your high-class junk mail and figure out what schemes were used. Notice the proportion of colors used. Sometimes just an accent of a color is added.

Look at the color combinations on buildings in your neighborhood, in your city, or when you travel. You will be most aware when you go somewhere new. We don't always see what's around us. For example, you probably drive

> Get up from where you are sitting now and go into the kitchen. Open the cupboard where you store canned goods and analyze the container labels. My oatmeal comes in a box with a triad color scheme, my tomatoes come in a can with a complementary scheme.

on "auto-pilot" to your local quilt store. Take a different route next time, and look at the buildings on the way.

Go to the library and look at magazines to see what colors the graphic artists put together for the articles. It's all out there, you just have to look. If you have trouble distinguishing slightly different colors from each other, go to the paint store and pick out some closely related color chips and bring them home to study them.

If you can't get to New York City to check out the newest color trends along Fifth Avenue, get in the car and go to the mall so you can anticipate what new colors are going to be in fashion. Like it or not, you will be seeing the colors in new fabrics at your quilt store and in quilt magazine ads. Be among the first to buy a fat quarter of the latest color.

MAKING CHOICES

Sometimes making color choices is a challenge. My sister and I spent weeks adjusting the colors before making a final decision on what colors to use when we had the exterior of our house repainted several years ago. The paint on a house will last a long time so you can't simply change your mind after the job is completed. Picking quilt colors can be just as challenging. I think of a prolific, elderly Amish quilter whose quilts I admire. Paul Pilgrim and Jerry Roy told me that she made her quilts like each wasn't her last. A good point to remember. Do the best you can on each quilt, learn what you can from it, then move on to the next one.

Have fun with color. Try some new colors with new color schemes and combinations. Be brave, experiment!

CHAPTER TWO

What's All the Fuss About Fabric?

As a group we quilters own tons of fabric. Are yours all similar or do you make an effort to buy different styles and colors of fabrics to add to your stash? In this chapter, I hope to make you more aware of the fabric you choose by studying some of the fabrics I buy.

COLLECTIONS

There are two kinds of fabric collections. Some collections are specifically designed to be used together. They are coordinated to have a common theme, feeling, and color scheme, but different motifs. Many quilt collections are designed by a famous-name designer who gets his or her name printed on the selvage along with the name of the collection. The fabric collection may even come in several colorways; different color versions of the same print.

The kind of collections I'm going to focus on are ones that are amassed over time, like art collections. Consciously, or unconsciously, many of us end up with collections of fabric in our stash that have to do with specific themes. I have Halloween, Christmas, cat, leaf, transportation, dot, stripe, paisley, Japanese, feed sack, and reproduction 30s collections, to name a few. It's fun to get out one of these groups of fabrics and actually use it.

Collections have a common subject matter, but otherwise they may be disparate. Individual fabrics may vary in color, scale, density of print, style of print, and so on. Let's look at examples from dot and stripes collections. You can clear your worktable and get out your dots and stripes. If you don't have dots or stripes, take out another collection. Use the categories on the following pages (Differences in Dots on page 17 and Differences in Stripes on page 19) or think of different categories to sort and divide your fabrics into.

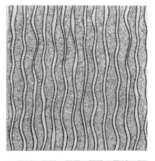
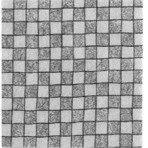

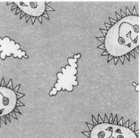
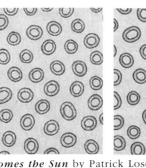
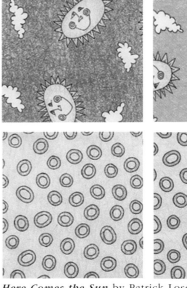

Here Comes the Sun by Patrick Lose.

Garage Doors. Berkeley, California. Photo by author. Learn to look for additional colorways of prints.

DIFFERENCES IN DOTS

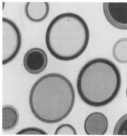
Busy

Calm

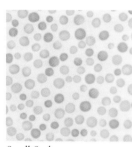
Small Scale

Large Scale

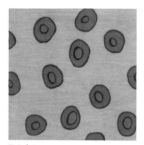
Bright

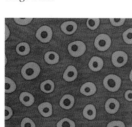
Subdued

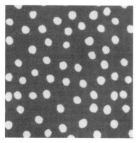
High Contrast

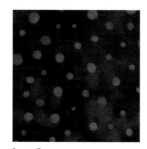
Low Contrast

What's Special About Dots?

Dots are small rounded shapes, spaced to form a pattern on fabric. The repetitive pattern catches our eye, particularly when there is high contrast between the dot and the background.

Pindots were one of the first new designs invented just for quilters that weren't based on historical fabric prints. Priscilla Miller hit the jackpot in the 70s when she introduced pindots for Concord Fabrics. They were small scale and appeared as two-color prints—usually white dots on a colored background. Now, other quilt fabric collections consist of many colorways of the same print just like the Pindot Collection did. Learn to look for this kind of collection and see how many versions you can include in one quilt.

Quilters have come a long way since pindots were introduced. Look at the differences between the dot fabrics pictured. Contrasting the dots in the chart with pindots, it becomes readily apparent that dots can be multicolored, differently sized, randomly placed, and not even perfectly round.

When I was building my large dot collection, I didn't know how I would use the fabrics, I just kept buying dots when I saw them. When I need some dots there will be similar-but-different ones to choose from. What doesn't get used returns to the collection.

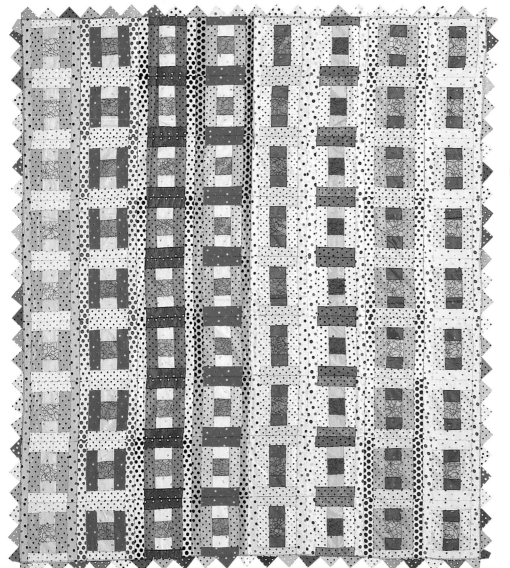

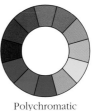

Back of taffeta dot log cabin quilt. Made from taffeta plaids.

To create a good, well-balanced collection of fabric you need to know what you already have. You also need to know what you should be looking for to add more variety.

Maybe you have included some dots in a quilt or two. It is also possible to create a quilt and limit yourself exclusively to dot fabrics. Six of the seven quilts in Chapter 9 (beginning on page 66) are dot quilts. However, we weren't the first to do this "dot only" thing. In the fall of 2001, Pat Gastor shared an antique taffeta dot quilt with me that she knew I would love. She was right, I loved it on sight! We both laughed at a shared memory of gathered, taffeta dress-up skirts we had worn as children.

Quilters weren't using multiple colorways of fabrics in quilts in the 1950s. Pat and I decided that the maker may have had access to a manufacturer's swatch books or scraps. This theory was reinforced when she showed me the back of the quilt.

Detail of Mostly Stripe Crazy Quilt.

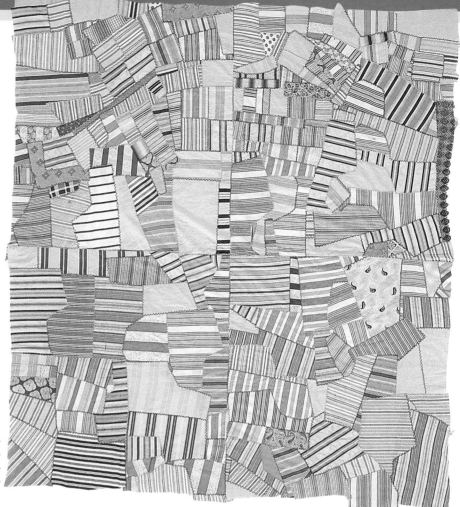

Polychromatic

*Mostly Stripe Crazy Quilt (*top).
Early 1900s. 75" x 82".
Maker unknown. Ohio.
Collection of the author.

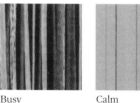

Busy   Calm

Large Scale   Small Scale

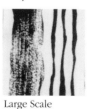

Bright   Subdued

High Contrast   Low Contrast

What's Special About Stripes?

I love stripes. So much in fact, I wrote a whole book about using stripe fabrics called *Stripes in Quilts*. I am a serious stripe collector. Six of the seven quilts in Chapter 10 (beginning on page 74) are stripe quilts. While the official definition of stripes is a linear pattern of lines that are parallel to each other, I amend it to say stripes are more or less straight lines running more or less parallel to each other. Repetitive lines of stripe fabrics move the eye along when we encounter them in a quilt. (People get confused, plaids are also a linear pattern, but their lines run perpendicular to each other. The crossed lines of plaids stop and trap the eye.)

There are more categories of stripes than dots. I came up with a couple dozen possible categories for *Stripes in Quilts*. Look at the stripe chart to see some of the ways stripes vary from each other.

I thought I was the first one to make a quilt using only stripe fabrics. I was wrong. The dealer who sold me the above quilt top figured I would find it in his quilt show booth because I had been buying stripe feed sacks from him for quite awhile.

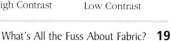

Do you see dandelions or dots?
Quebec, Canada. Photo by author.

Do you see dandelions or stripes?
Quebec, Canada. Photo by author.

Variety is the spice of life. Learn to put more variety into your quilts, even if you work with only one type of print in a quilt. Try evaluating one of your collections by dividing the fabrics into categories, as I have with my dots and stripes. You'll know your fabrics a lot better when you're done, and you'll be more aware of what you need to add to the collection.

What's Special About Batiks

Solid colors provide a resting spot for the eye when you look at quilts. Many quilters would prefer to use batiks, hand-dyes, and hand-dyed look-alikes. One of the problems with these fabrics is that what makes them beautiful can also make them hard to use. They are streaky and ethereal, their lack of solidity confuses the issue when they're cut up in small pieces and sewn back together. It can be hard to tell where one fabric ends and another begins in pieced blocks.

A little bit is okay; too much looks like mush.

Let's look at some samples that combine batiks with my also-busy leaf collection. The simple star, called Naoko Star, is made from four two-piece units. Since many batik lovers like to include lots of different pieces of fabric, I did the same. I needed sixteen leaf prints and sixteen batiks. (I was one short on a yellow batik, but I *almost* made it.) The first sample on the next page has batik stars and leaf backgrounds. I reversed this in the second sample. I used the same set of fabrics in the same block position in both samples.

It is easier to pick out the stars in the second sample. We will be learning more about positive and negative space in the next chapter, but simply put, the leaf prints are too strong to remain in the background (negative space) in the first sample. There is just too much to take in. A word of warning to

quilters who switch into the automatic-cutting mode. Sometimes, it is wiser to cut a couple of sample blocks, arrange them on the design wall, step back, and evaluate what is going on. Take control over the design process and become an active participant.

A third batik/leaf sample, the tilted or askew squares showcase my leaf prints. The beautiful batik prints have been relegated to a background role. The fabrics seem to be blended and happy. And whether you realize it or not, you have been studying three polychromatic color schemes!

Quilters love to buy fabric. It helps to make sense out of what you have amassed so you can make more interesting quilts. Really looking at your fabric not only tells you what you like, it also makes you more aware of what you should consider adding.

Batik stars + leaf backgrounds

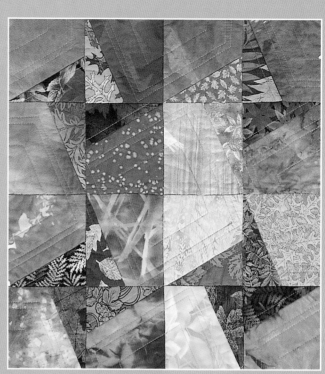

Leaf stars + batik backgrounds

Leaf squares + batik backgrounds

CHAPTER THREE

What's All the Fuss About Design?

In the previous two chapters I have discussed color and fabric. There are a lot of different ways to put the two together in a quilt. In this chapter I'm going to try to isolate some of the things that I'm particularly aware of that go into designing good quilts. Most likely you have heard of the design principles and elements, you may even have memorized a list of them in school. As a quilter, you want to know how they apply to the quilts you make, so I'll give you some examples. Then, I will go a step further and add some personal hints that I have found helpful in using good design when making quilts.

I have been a quilter for over thirty years and have decided that quilters make up a personal set of rules when they make a quilt, although they may not realize it. The rules guide their choices as they go along. I will show you how this idea works in practice.

DESIGN PRINCIPLES

The design principles are a universally agreed upon set of ideas that can be applied to creating and evaluating art.

BALANCE creates a sense of equilibrium between the parts of a quilt. Without it, the design seems unstable. Many quilters in the United States intuitively make symmetrical quilts because they feel balanced. In other words, if there are four corner blocks, we think they should all be the same color. A quilt can be balanced even if each border or each corner is a different fabric. You might just have to move the pieces around until it feels intuitively balanced. It's fun to stretch and try finding balance among non-identical things.

PROPORTION is how the parts of a quilt relate to each other as a whole. For example, structurally the size of the quilt border should feel comfortable with the center of the quilt. Proportion can also apply to color. When you choose a color scheme, you don't have to use equal amounts of each color.

RHYTHM is what ties the units of a design together. It creates a path for your eye to follow as you take in the quilt. Repetition of lines, shapes, colors, and fabrics provide this rhythm.

EMPHASIS is about dominance and subordination. You need both. In allover designs, we have to find a balance between keeping it simple and making it boring.

DESIGN ELEMENTS

The design elements are like the ingredients in a recipe. Two recipes may have similar ingredients but they are combined in different ways and produce different results.

COLOR is important to how you perceive quilts. You love some colors and dislike others. You can use color schemes as a guide to help you select colors for a new quilt or for coming up with new combinations of colors to try.

The SHAPES of the pieces in the block create silhouettes of positive and negative spaces when they are filled with different value fabrics. A lot of quilters don't pay much attention to negative (background) space because it is the leftover space in a block. With the right fabric selection, it can be exciting!

Straight and curved LINES create the map or "bones" of the quilt. The repeated lines of the sashing or borders tie the parts of the quilt together.

TEXTURE in quilts can be achieved by using three-dimensional fabric manipulations or by using contrasting fabric patterning.

REPETITION occurs in traditional repeat block quilts, like the repeat block quilts I have selected for the book. The elements of design work to unify the quilt. Our challenge is to learn how to keep repetition from getting monotonous. Using an odd number of elements can help prevent monotony.

Repetition ties a composition together. Tourist Cottages. Quebec, Canada. Photo by author.

VALUE is the lightness or darkness of the colors. Value contrast between the pieces that make up blocks helps us to distinguish block patterns.

SIZE is relative. Big blocks show off the pattern of fabrics differently than the same blocks created in a smaller size. Sometimes you need to change the block size to accommodate a particular print. Repeating consistent block dimensions also works to tie the quilt together.

The shape of a quilt gives it a feeling of DIRECTION. Changing the direction of the way blocks are placed changes how we perceive a quilt. Horizontal quilts "feel" different than vertical quilts. Distributing the colors in a diagonal or zigzag pattern across blocks gives a feeling of more energy than having it distributed in restful horizontal rows or evenly from block to block.

Designing is making choices. This chapter is about taking control of what is happening in your quilt. I'll begin by sharing some things you might not have considered.

Viewing Distances

Every quilt has three viewing distances that you can use to evaluate how effective the design is. The distance between you and the quilt affects how you perceive it. Try to make your quilts so the viewer will have something to see at each of the three distances.

"Across a crowded room" is where the graphic qualities really speak out. The Best of Show in many quilt shows is an "across a crowded room" quilt. Some lovely quilts are too subtle to be strong at this distance.

Cloud truck, "across a crowded room" distance. Berkeley, California. Photo by the author

Cloud truck, "aisle viewing" distance. Berkeley, California. Photo by the author.

Cloud truck, "up close and personal." Berkeley, California. Photo by the author.

"4'-8' aisle-viewing distance" is an intermediate range where we begin to see more specific details. All quilts should look good here.

"Up close and personal" is where you really notice fabric and construction details. Try to have a gift to the viewer here. It could be good workmanship, fine quilting, interesting threads, unusual fabrics, embellishments, and so on.

Activity Level

I sometimes refer to the activity level of the quilt. It's one of my design terms, which relates to how busy or calm the quilt feels. We have the power to change the activity level by choosing fabrics that support the activity level we want.

Making Order in the Chaos

Another of my pet terms is "making order in the chaos." Sometimes your quilt might seem to "run away with you," when there is too much happening at once, but you don't know where to begin to correct it. This often happens because you weren't clear on the "rules" (page 25) when you started, and your mind wandered somewhere along the way. Having some clear design rules will give you a checklist to help you figure out how to get out of the muddle you've gotten yourself into.

DESIGN HINTS

I decided it would be helpful to point out design tidbits about different quilts. Design doesn't happen in a vacuum, so I'm including "Design Hints" as I go along in the narration of the book. These little handy hints will mean the most when they apply to a specific quilt you might be looking at and studying. Then you will be more aware of how you can consciously make design decisions about what is going on in your own quilts.

DECIDING ON RULES

All quilts have rules, or design guidelines. In the last two chapters I discussed ways that fabric and color choices become a part of the end product, but what else is involved?

Making Rules for a Simple Quilt

Let's begin with a relatively uncomplicated vintage quilt top and see if we can figure out some rules. Ann Rhode recently found this top made by her Aunt Helen, who pieced it with scraps found in the closet of Ann's mother Marion Smith Bishop. The top is a straight-forward, use-it-up and make-do kind of quilt. I can be very detailed and come up with eight rules:

Rule #1: Scrap = multi-fabric, anything goes

Rule #2: Scrap = multicolored

Rule #3: Squares = cut 10" x 10"

Rule #4: Sashing = cut squares 3½" x 3½"

Pieced top. 70" x 87½". 1958. Helen Bailey, Atlantic City, Iowa. In the collection of Ann A. Rhode.

Rule #5: Sashing = run one way only

Rule #6: Sashing = add bright pink squares

Rule #7: Border = repeat 3½" squares

Rule #8: Border = bright pink corners only

Rule #6 for Helen's quilt is the most interesting. She made an effort to make the multicolored, multi-square sashing stronger visually by including repeated bright pink squares. The bright pink squares in the border that runs around the quilt, highlight, or anchor, the four corners.

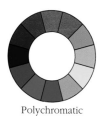

Polychromatic

DESIGN HINTS
- Multiple printed fabrics raise the activity level of the quilt.
- Simple blocks lower the activity level of the quilt.

Making Rules for
Pieced Blocks

I just gave you rules for a quilt that was made up of squares, but most pieced quilts have more complicated blocks. Whenever you have a variety of fabrics, colors and shapes, you need rules to keep them organized.

A pieced block has a set of variables or "zones." For example, a star block has two zones, the background and the star. Once you figure out what the zones are, you get to pick what type of fabric or color to put in each. This allows you to take control, to create order in the chaos. If the quilt runs away with you, you can refer to the rules one by one, see where you strayed, and get yourself back on track.

Churn Dash blocks. Using many colors isn't as calm as using few colors.

CHURN DASH OR HOLE
IN THE BARN DOOR

Let's start with something simple and straight forward. The negative space in some blocks is easy to figure out. Churn Dash, or Hole in the Barn Door as the Amish call it, is one such block.

The block has two variables or zones, so there are just two color choices to make for each block.

Contrast *Hole in the Barn Door* quilt with the colorful blocks in the glued mock-up sample above. There's a lot more to take in here. Even though the colors are solids, the sample is not as calm as my Amish quilt.

Rule #1: Color = multi for blocks and
 alternate blocks
Rule #2: Blocks = all blocks different
 two-color combinations
Rule #3: Alternate blocks =
 all different

Polychromatic

DESIGN HINT
• Using more colors raises
 the activity level of a quilt.

What's most interesting about *Hole in the Barn Door* is that the quiltmaker probably ran out of fabric and had to figure out what to do with the three odd blocks made with alternate fabrics. There are a lot of ways to handle running out of fabric.

Rule #1: Color = two color

Rule #2: Block positive space = beige

Rule #3: Block negative space = black

Rule #4: Alternate plain blocks = beige

Rule #5: Narrow border = black

Rule #6: Wide border = beige

Hole in the Barn Door. 70" x 78". 20th Century. Ohio Amish.
Collection of the author. .

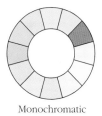

Monochromatic

DESIGN HINTS
• Solids are calming.
• The fewer the
  colors, the calmer
  the effect.

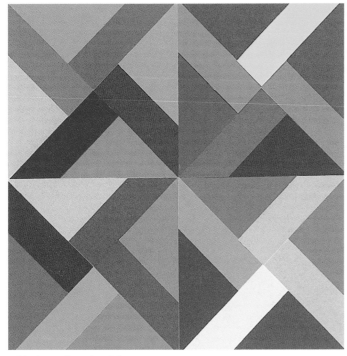

X blocks made with solids.

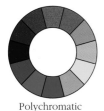

Polychromatic

DESIGN HINT
• Although solids are calmer than prints, using lots of solids raises the activity level.

X Block

A number of years ago I saw a very poor quality picture of an antique quilt made using X blocks, pieced in mostly medium to medium-dark solids, that has haunted me ever since. The X Block is another simple block that illustrates how you can really change the design of your quilt by your fabric and color choices.

The X forms the positive space and the triangles form the leftover negative space. While there are only two templates, you can end up with many variables if you don't confine yourself to making two-color blocks.

First, I tried making a glued mock-up as a reminder of the antique quilt. There was really only one rule to follow:

Rule #1: Place any color anywhere, but not next to itself.

Then I moved on to subtle. I had a set of pushed-neutrals: four blues and four neutrals to use in the blocks. There were enough colors to make four different two-color blocks but that would be obvious, so I came up with these rules:

Rule #1: Colors = all eight colors in each block

Rule #2: Colors = group blues, group neutrals by zone

Rule #3: "X" pieces = two blues + two neutrals

Rule #4: Background = just opposite of Rule #3

Pushed-Neutrals

DESIGN HINT
• Subtle doesn't have to be boring. Use lots of subtle fabrics to raise the activity level.

Subtle X Blocks.

Cat fabrics can be used in the background negative space rather than in the foreground positive space.

Now I was warmed up, so I decided to see what I could do with my collection of cat prints. It is hard to cut up such busy prints. You don't see the prints unless you are up close, so you might feel they are wasted.

Sorting through my fabrics, I picked out prints with dark backgrounds because there was less contrast between the cats and the background color. Relatively speaking, they weren't as "spotty" as the white background prints where there was more contrast between the motifs and the background.

Polychromatic

DESIGN HINTS
- Busy, "crayon-box-bright" prints raise the activity level.
- When using a one-way print (cats all stand one way) it works best to cut the four triangles from a square. Then all the cats will be happy.

Rule #1: Block = two color

Rule #2: Block = different prints in each

Rule #3: Negative space triangles = cats

Rule #4: "X" pieces = one color, but four different prints

The cat fabrics are cheerful, to say the least. They would be perfect for a child's quilt. Challenge yourself to learn something about color and design even when you are making light-hearted projects.

Blocks intuitively arranged.
Rebecca Rohrkaste.

Blocks arranged with rules + intuition.
Mary Mashuta.

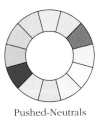

Pushed-Neutrals

NAOKO STAR

Let's look at the Naoko Star from Chapter 2 (page 21) again. There, I used batiks and leaf fabrics. As you might remember, there are two variables, or zones: the star and the background. However, there are eight positions in the block to fill. (I used eight fabrics last time.) I had Rebecca Rohrkast arrange a set of pushed neutrals in one set of four blocks. She looked, she pondered, she moved pieces around until she was pleased.

While Rebecca composed her blocks intuitively, I made up rules to help me begin to compose my blocks. I used intuition, but I had rules to get me started. Using rules is one of the ways you can move toward becoming more artful.

This might be hard for many quilters to do, so I made up some rules about what to place where.

Rule #1: Blocks = eight colors in each

Rule #2: Blocks = none alike

Rule #3: Stars = two blue, two neutral

Rule #4: Negative space = opposite of star color

Naoko Stripes. 1996. Mary Mashuta.

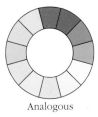

Analogous

I originally came up with Naoko Star to showcase three Japanese stripes that are on permanent loan from Naoko Anne Ito. I made them into an outfit for the American Quilter's Society Fashion Show.

Rule #1: Stars = many reds

Rule #2: Negative space = same stripe in four adjoining block corners

Rule #3: Negative space = alternate orientation of stripe lines so a woven effect is created

Rule #4: Negative space = diagonal rows of stripe corners

Rule #4 was a good way to have the blocks look less clunky in the jacket.

The design principles and elements give you a vocabulary to use to build, discuss, and compare quilts. Much of what you do as a quilter may be intuitive, but sometimes you need to step back and interpret what is going on in a quilt, particularly if it isn't pleasing you.

CHAPTER FOUR

Thinking Outside the Box

Now that you are more aware of the positive (foreground) and negative (background) space in individual blocks, let's move on to designing whole quilts. Backgrounds are afterthoughts for many quilters. You can learn to make them more interesting. To begin, it is easier if you think of the positive space and the negative space as two separate chapters in the book you are reading. While they relate to each other, you can't read both at the same time.

Learn to look beyond the positive space. Republic Bank, Houston, Texas. Photo by author.

ALTERING TRADITIONAL BACKGROUNDS

Let's look at some quilts where negative space plays an important part in the overall design of the quilt.

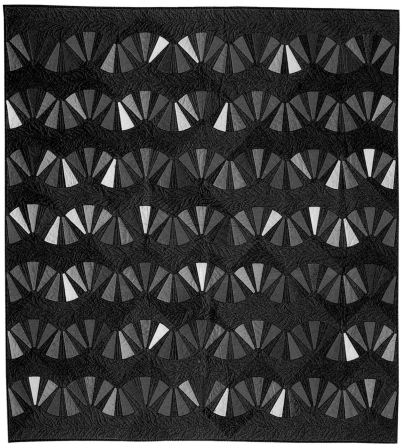

Fans. 84" x 79". 1992. Mabry Benson, Kensington, California.

FAN QUILT

Mabry Benson tampered with the background of the Fan block and made her quilt look more contemporary. In a traditional rendering of the quilt, the multi-color fans would be placed on a one-color, contrasting background like muslin.

Rule #1: Background = purple solid

Rule #2: Fan wedges = polychromatic solids

Rule #3: Alternating fan wedges = purple solid

Repeating the purple negative space in half of the fan wedges causes the purple parts of the quilt to visually fuse together. Mabry's serpentine fans seem to float above the background.

Polychromatic

DESIGN HINT
• Bright colors contrast against a dark background and pop forward.

Background for Appliqué

In realistic appliqué you usually spend a lot of time thinking about the subject matter, but the background is also an important consideration.

For years, I tried to figure out how to portray one of my favorite restaurants in a quilt. Finally, I moved a floral plaid from the back to the front of the quilt. A semi-realistic scene helps overcome the bold floral in the background because it catches the viewer's eye and brings it to the center of the quilt. The plaid is not the first thing you see.

DESIGN HINT
• The clerk was rather casual in cutting my floral plaid fabric. When unfolded, her cut caused the fabric to form a "V". The lines helped to draw the viewer's eye into the quilt.

Breakfast at Cafe Beaujolais. 40½" x 57". 1990. Mary Mashuta.

Reflections of Athens. 46" x 51". 1996. Kathy Sward, Muir Beach, California

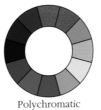

Polychromatic

DESIGN HINT
• A palette softer than the foreground geranium and window frame keeps the view in the background.

Background View

Kathy Sward found another way to show us background. This time it is viewed through a window. She remembered how the sun lit hillside buildings in Athens. She saw light, shadows, and reflections and was able to create the feeling of the scene without being realistic.

Background Grids

Developing a background grid may be a stretch, but it's fun once you get the hang of it. The simplest grid is a checkerboard. You just need one stripe or two colors to alternate. Once you understand the concept, you can learn to make grids more interesting. Start looking for more complex grids.

One-Stripe Grid

Two-Color Grid. Adelaide Mashuta.

Analogous grid made from magazine pictures.

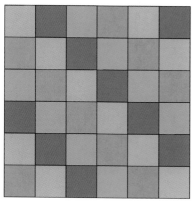

Stair-Step Grid

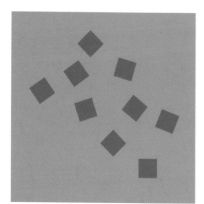

Contemporary grid floats on background. Adelaide Mashuta.

Multicolor tile grid. Apartment Building. Berkeley, California. Photo by author.

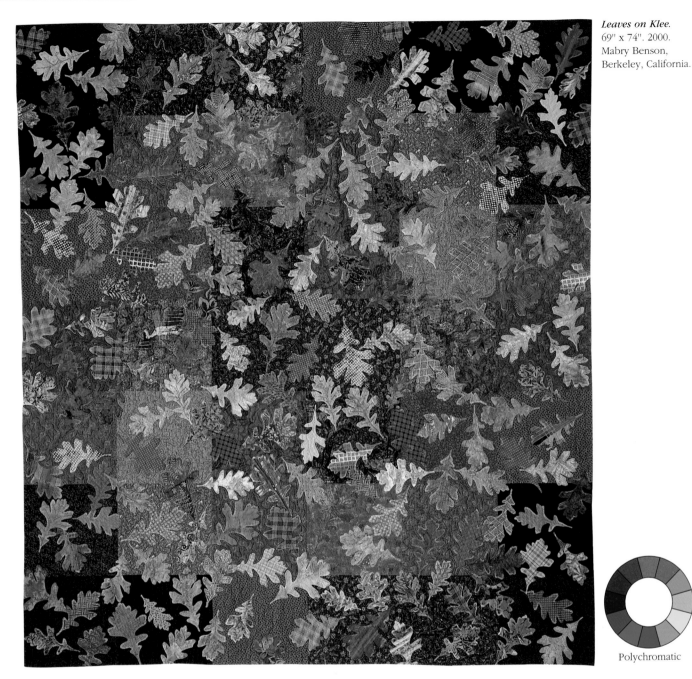

Leaves on Klee.
69" x 74". 2000.
Mabry Benson,
Berkeley, California.

Polychromatic

Grids for Appliqué

Let's look at two leaf appliqué quilts that use grid backgrounds.

LEAF QUILT

Mabry Benson collected fall leaves on a trip to the East Coast. You are most aware of the beautiful leaf shapes when you look at Mabry's quilt from a distance. As you move closer, however, the multicolored grid pattern behind the leaves emerges. Notice how Mabry has kept the grid fairly dark, except for a few muted red accents.

Rule #1: Leaves = fall colors

Rule #2: Background grid = random darker colors with red accents

Rule #3: Background grid = arrange darker blocks to act as a frame

DESIGN HINTS
- Place accent colors toward the center of the grid so your eye doesn't wander.
- Mabry remembered the "gift to the viewer" and machine stitched her appliquéd leaves using random zigzag stitches with variegated thread.

ANOTHER LEAF QUILT

I had the honor of taking a class from Dorr Bothwell at the Mendocino Art Center (she taught at the Chicago Art Institute for many years). I used her idea of a half-drop grid when I wanted to do a simple leaf quilt. The half-drop grid is a little more subtle than the stair-step grid. Both create a diagonal background.

Rule #1: Leaves = fall colors

Rule #2: Background grid = half-drop

Rule #3: Background grid = subtle beige and gray prints

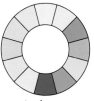

Analogous

Leaves. Unfinished top, late 1980s. Mary Mashuta. Two-color half-drop grid.

DOUBLE WEDDING RING

Mary Russell makes Double Wedding Ring quilts. The quilt has two variables: rings and background. Traditionally the rings would all be pieced to a one-color background, which was often muslin. Rule #4 was sneaky and she was artful with Rule #5. Can you find the border that has two square on squares rather than just one?

Polychromatic

Rule #1: Rings = primary or secondary color in assorted prints but limited to one color within block

Rule #2: Background = complement of ring color in "wispy-colored" solid

Rule #3: Intersections = Four-Patch from wispy-colored solids

Rule #4: Small inner border = complementary strips determined by what is either diagonally or right across from piece

Rule #5: Outer-border circles on squares = paired warm color with cool color

DESIGN HINT

• Working in a series allows you to concentrate on growing artistically because you don't have to reinvent the wheel every time you begin a new project.

Complementary Colors. 42" x 57½". 1998. Mary Russell, San Luis Obispo, California.

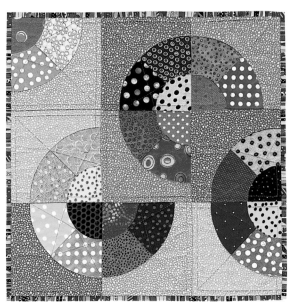

Colorway Dots. 19" x 19". 1999. Mary Mashuta.

Polychromatic

Stop, Look, and Listen. 24½" x 31½". 1999. Mary Mashuta.

Turning Pieced Blocks into Grids

If there is substantial negative space along the edge of a pieced block, the block can be used to create a grid pattern.

Alternate blocks can be colored differently like some of the samples you were studying. The traditional Circle within Circle block has all negative space at the edge of the block. However, I divided the one-fabric background into four squares so I could use more fabrics. (We will be studying this block further in Chapter 9, beginning on page 66.)

SCHOOL PROJECT

When Pat Morris and Jeannette Muir asked me to make a quilt for the exhibit "Tactile Academics:...Quilt-makers Go Back to School" I got out my collection of Driver's Ed fabrics.

It would have been more ordinary to place the red and blue prints in the circles, but I would still have to alternate them with something else or they would have mushed together.

Rule #1: Rings = beige/gray wedges + black-and-white car print

Rule #2: Centers = three stoplight colors in one-color dot groupings

Rule #3: Background corners = assorted red or blue back-ground car fabrics

MULTIPLE COLORWAYS

In Chapter 2 we talked about looking for and buying multiple colorways of a fabric. I am hooked on this idea, so I often buy "less of more" rather than "more of less." You still end up with the same amount of yardage.

In multiple colorways the pattern is constant. The negative space is the perfect place for them because pattern doesn't change, just the color does. The background has an allover uniformity about it. A grid can be created with just two alternating versions, but it's fun to use more.

Rule #1: Wedges = multiple dots

Rule #2: Quarter-circles = multiple dots

Rule #3: Background corners = 4 colorways of dot placed randomly

CREATING ALLOVER BLOCKS WITH COLOR AND FABRIC

I am always looking for simple blocks to use in classes because I have students of varying backgrounds and skill levels. I like to teach about color, fabric selection, and design, not about complicated construction. I enjoy searching through books filled with illustrations of quilt blocks. I am always on the lookout for blocks that can change optically when stitched to a sister block.

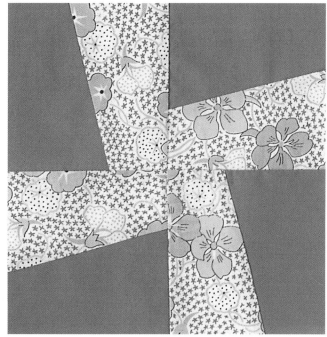

A. Windmill block with one-color background.

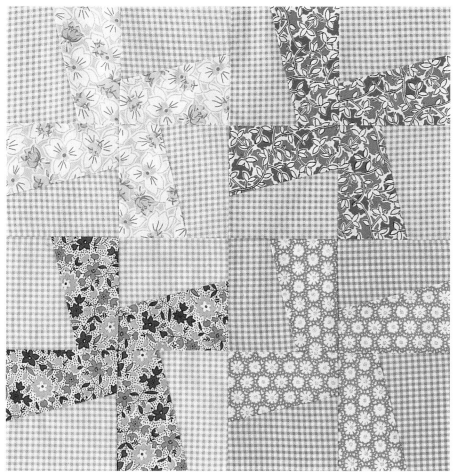

B. Four Windmill blocks with four different color backgrounds.

Windmill A and Windmill B

Windmill is such a block. It only requires one template. Four identical units are stitched to create the windmill in the center of the block.

Rule #1: Positive space
    blades = 30s prints

Rule #2: Negative space
    blades = solid

I got adventuresome realizing I could use different colorways to create a different look by changing Rule #2.

New Rule #2: Negative space blades
    = different check
    colorway for each
    block

The leftover corners also have the potential of becoming windmills if combined with three matching partners in adjoining units.

Windmill C

If you look at the middle of Sample B (page 37) where four different color checks touch as the blocks join, you will see that an intermediate block, or tessellation, could be created there. All you would have to do is use checks all the same color! The blocks will no longer read as individual blocks, they will become an overall or continuous design.

New Rule #2: Negative space blades = same color check in four adjoining corners

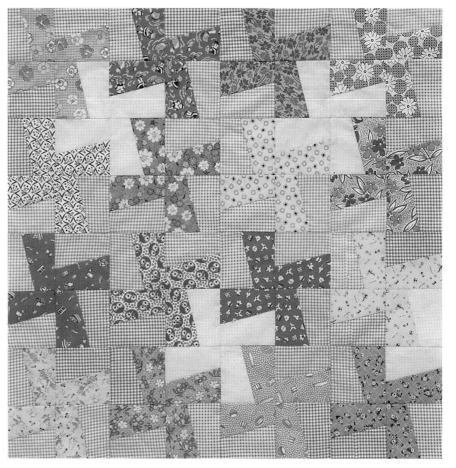

C. *16-block Windmill* (top). 32"x 32". Mary Mashuta

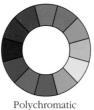

Polychromatic

Windmill D

Pat Hastings tried the Windmill block, too. She found another solution for the negative space and she created a border that floats the windmills.

New Rule #2: Negative space blades = 30s solids

New Rule #3: Border = half pinwheel blocks cut from same print + same print strip

D. *Windmill.* 45½" x 54". 2002. Patricia B. Hastings, Stevensville, Montana.

CREATING NEW RULES

Sometimes a quilt has interesting design rules that are only readily apparent to the designer. I enjoy asking when I can't figure things out. If the maker begins the explanation with the phrase, "well now, of course…" I know I will be told something that probably wouldn't have dawned on me.

George Taylor and I each made a Wagon Wheel quilt, each following our own rules.

George Taylor's quilt is the traditional reading of the block. His spokes float on the plain background. My version emphasizes the individual blocks rather than being an allover grid. I catch the viewer's eye with color changes.

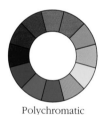

Polychromatic

Blue Wagon Wheel. 51½" x 72½". 1999. George Taylor, Anchorage, Alaska.

Check Wagon Wheel. 38" x 36½". 2000. Mary Mashuta.

Blue Wagon Wheel

Rule #1: Block spokes = multiple feed sack prints

Rule #2: Block negative space spokes = muslin

Rule #3: Center circles = blue

Check Wagon Wheel

Rule #1: Block spokes = one-color reproduction 30s prints for each

Rule #2: Block negative space spokes = one-colorway check for each that matches color of prints

Rule #3: Center circle = multicolored solids

Polychromatic

Hot Stripes and Cool Dots.
41½" x 42 ½". 2002.
Julie Anderson,
Palo Alto, California.

Julie Anderson had seen our quilts and was able to think outside the box. She kept talking to me about corners, but I didn't get it. For her, the traditional hexagon block became the way the quilt was constructed, not the way it was viewed! She saw different connections between the blocks than I did.

Rule #1: Block spokes = two spokes from adjoining blocks are cut from same stripe, but spokes within a block not necessarily the same

Rule #2: Block negative space spokes = three from adjoining blocks cut from same dot

Rule #3: Center circle = multicolored chambray-weave solids

Julie is a master of contrast: colors to their complements; warm colors to cool colors; linear stripes to rounded dots. And, if that weren't enough, she arranged the background in a color flow that softens the contrasts she created.

Julie didn't compose her quilt in a day; once she had her rules she was able to work on it over an extended period of time. All the hours were worth it as far as I'm concerned! Julie Anderson gets our minds spinning in different directions, ready to see new things.

The background parts of blocks often add little to the finished quilt because quilters concentrate on making the positive space interesting and/or beautiful. Now you know that the negative space is just one more zone to include in your planning process. Background is background, but it can be interesting, too.

CHAPTER FIVE

Getting Ready

I've discussed color, fabric, design, and thinking
outside the box in previous chapters.
Before I turn you loose on the six blocks I've
selected for projects, let's talk about some things
that may make your work easier.

WHAT'S ALL THE FUSS ABOUT BEING ARTFUL?

Being artful is a term that means pushing the ordinary, commonly
accepted, and understood. It means going beyond the easily accessible,
and stretching and growing.

There are basically two kinds of quilts: "generated" quilts and
"composed" quilts. Some quilters like to make generated quilts because
the teacher or author gives them a formula and tells them exactly what to
do so they don't have to worry about making decisions. They cut and
stitch, so much of this and so much of that. When they're done, they have
a quilt. I want my students to compose their own quilts because I would
prefer to let them figure out their own right answers. I give them blocks,
some guidelines, maybe some rules, and always some hints. The quilts
featured in the following chapters were all composed—rather than
generated—by their makers.

MOVING FROM THE FLOOR TO THE WALL

In the past, quilters didn't have quilt studios. If we wanted to see
what the stitched blocks looked like before they were joined, we spread
the blocks out on the floor or laid them out on the bed. When I became a
quilter in the early 1970s I worked on a table while I cut and machine
stitched my quilts. If I wanted to see the blocks or pieces together, I
spread them out on the floor. This seemed only natural as I had always
cut garments out on the living room floor.

When "art" quilters joined the ranks of traditional quilters, they began
laying out their quilts on "design walls," which were anything from pieces
of Pellon fleece taped to a handy wall, to permanently installed and ele-
gantly finished vertical work surfaces. When you create your quilt on a
design wall you don't have to make instant decisions, you give yourself
time to think and ponder, you move pieces around, you take them down
and put them back, you let them sit in place overnight and then see if you
want to make changes in the morning. Artists refer to this process as
"revision." Sometimes you have to suffer, but eventually things feel right
and you are ready to move forward to construction.

COMPOSING ALLOVER AND CONTINUOUS DESIGNS

The six blocks presented in this book are traditional blocks and have block names. They are made up of units and form all-over designs. Often, pieces in one unit connect optically to pieces in another unit, which actually may be part of another block. Circle within Circle and Serpentine Curves form interconnecting designs between the units. Even Air Ship Propeller, which is sewn like a traditional block, has parts that connect to the blocks around it.

How you see them is not how they are sewn. Many quilters are accustomed to stitching their blocks and then moving the stitched blocks around on their design wall before they finally sew them together. The blocks in this book don't work like this because the way each block is composed relates directly to what is happening in the adjoining blocks. Pinwheel, Double Stars, Triple Pinwheels, Circle within Circle, and Serpentine Curves are stitched in units rather than as whole blocks. The units for these all-over designs can't be stitched until the whole design is figured out. You have to compose first and stitch second.

I don't sew my blocks or quilts until they are entirely composed on a design wall, which may be a new thought for you to absorb. None of us likes to rip out stitches, and seams make very final statements once they are stitched. Not immediately sewing gives me an opportunity to think about the quilt over a period of time, to move pieces around, and to make substitutions.

Installing a design wall in your home will make composing your quilts much easier. You will also have a place to park the pieces and parts while the quilt is being created.

If all this design talk makes you nervous, don't worry. All the blocks are relatively simple and easily stitched. I'll be showing and telling you how other quilters made their quilts. There are also quilt projects, templates, and cutting and sewing directions at the back of the book that you will help you get started.

CREATING A DESIGN WALL

I began teaching Designing Workspaces workshops in the 1980s when I became a full-time quilter. The class has been offered at shops and conferences across the United States.

Without exception, the number one item quilters want in their workroom is a design wall. You have probably used Pellon fleece, Thermo Lamb, or a flannel-backed vinyl tablecloth in a workshop as a temporary design wall. Sometimes you tape it to the wall or pin it to a drapery.

Some prefer to pin it to a foamcore board (thin, lightweight material available at art supply stores). Quilters usually buy 4' x 4' or 4' x 8' sheets. You may even own a piece of foamcore that you take to workshops. Are you ready for a more permanent solution?

Celotex is a soft fiberboard used in soundproofing that can be permanently installed on your wall. Purchase two 4' x 8' x ¾" sheets so you end up with an 8' x 8' design area. They do need to be fixed to your wall. If you only lean the sheets against the wall like you do foamcore, they will eventually buckle.

WHERE ARE YOU GOING TO PUT YOUR DESIGN WALL?

Your first challenge is finding a 8' x 8' space for it. I have found that most quilters never have enough space, no matter how much space they have. We have to learn to use our space more efficiently. You will have to look critically. Are there any 8' areas that are unbroken by doors, windows, or built-ins? What can you move or toss? Can you replace two 4' high bookcases with one 8' high?

To help clear the clutter, my students make an "alternative placement" list of stuff they can relocate or get rid of. Sometimes it involves stuff in other rooms and/or other family member's possessions. There may be a ripple effect before you can claim your space.

If you have a choice between two walls, locate your design wall where it is most easily seen from where you cut and sew. Hopefully you can stand back and get a good look. Remember that quilts have three viewing distances: across a crowded room, 4'-8' aisle viewing distance, and up close and personal. If you can't step back and look, you might really be shocked when

your quilt is hung in your local quilt show or in your living room. (In a pinch, buy a reducing glass which works as a reverse magnifying glass.)

INSTALLING YOUR DESIGN WALL

There are many ways to install a design wall, just like there are many ways to make a quilt. Here is what Jerry Bedsole and I devised.

1. You will need "nailers" (long strips of wood to nail the Celotex to), ½" or 1" x 2" x 8' will most likely work. Check to see if there is a top or bottom room molding. Its width will determine the depth of the nailers. You will need six nailers, but subtract for molding(s) that will act as nailers.
2. Nail the nailers into the wall studs.
3. Nail the Celotex to the nailers using small nails. Remember to space the nails across each strip, not just at the ends.
4. Cover the Celotex with fabric using a staple gun.
5. Apply molding to the edges of your design wall using finish nails. Mitered corners look nice.
6. You may also want to affix additional thin strips of molding to edges that can be seen from the side.

Jerry secures the nailers into the studs. Photos by author.

Jerry positions a sheet of Celotex before nailing it into the nailers.

Roberta positions the first layer of decorator felt while Jerry holds a piece of molding parallel to the edge of the design wall as a guide.

Roberta begins a project on her new design wall.

SELECTING A DESIGN WALL COVERING

It's not necessary to cover your design wall with fabric, but it looks a lot nicer. The same goes for adding molding. There are a number of fabrics that can be used as a covering for your design wall.

For a seamless covering you can use 3 yards of 108" wide muslin, or a king-size 108" x 102" flannel sheet. Fabric pieces won't cling to muslin, but they will to flannel.

Jerry and I used decorator felt from a drapery store. I like to install a double-thickness because it's easier to pin into a cushioned surface. I purchased three 8' cuts of 60"-wide felt. The third section was cut in half lengthwise so I ended up with two half-strips. We attached one layer of one-and-a-half strips vertically and the other layer horizontally so the "joins" were in different places. I used white-headed glass pins where the pieces butted in the center areas because they show a lot less than staples. You will probably want to steam your covering to remove wrinkles and fold lines. Smooth the fabric as you stretch it over the Celotex. Staple the top and bottom first, and then the sides.

Now you are aware of the things I think are important to consider when you want to make more visually interesting quilts. Your studio and fabrics are ready. Composing your own quilt is an exciting process! Have fun studying the quilts and be sure to pick a block or two to try yourself.

Detail of *Repro Propellers*. 39" x 38". 2002. Patricia Deforce, Oakland, California. Quilted by Kari Ruedisale, Lansing, Michigan.

CHAPTER SIX

Pinwheel

Unusual border fabrics can add a lot to a quilt. Learn to think outside the box. Storefront, Berkeley, California. Photo by author.

Let's begin with a simple one-template block. Pinwheel has a lot in common with the one-template Windmill block discussed in Chapter 4 (pages 37-38). I find it a little more graceful. "Which to put where?" is eliminated in both blocks.

Pinwheel is an example of "how you see it is not how you sew it." Visually, four same-fabric pieces in adjoining units join to create the pinwheel. All the pinwheels are potentially of equal importance: there is no negative space, just continuous pinwheels.

For the viewer to make sense of the quilt, each pinwheel in this overall design needs to stand on its own against the other pinwheels that surround it. Sometimes it is necessary to move a pinwheel to another position where there is more color contrast, more value contrast, and/or more pattern contrast. (Since you haven't sewn anything together, it's no big deal.) This auditioning process is fun. Keep working until things feel right.

Repetition works to your advantage. Placing multiple same-color pinwheels in your composition helps to move the eye around the quilt. The pinwheels don't have to be exactly the same color or fabric. More is better, and a lot more fun.

Sometimes, one color or print in particular seems to stand out. Make sure it is repeated so it won't act as a bull's-eye.

Pinwheel is a simple quilt block and a good place to start in designing your own quilt. However, there are many ways to treat the blocks at the border of the quilt. Be sure to look at the border treatments as you study the following quilts. There are five solutions offered.

Pinwheel is a good block to show off a good assortment of different kinds of fabric since contrast of color and print type is important. The block makes a perfect allover design for wearables as you will see at the end of the chapter.

THERE ARE FIVE EDGE OPTIONS FOR THIS QUILT:

No border	=	partial pinwheels at the edge as units completed
Frame	=	unpieced, one-fabric border
Frame	=	unpieced, one-fabric border + corner blocks
Frame	=	several random "completed" pinwheels made using two templates put together to form one template. This large pinwheel shape plus one pinwheel piece are cut from border fabric.
All pinwheels completed	=	extras "float" on pieced one-fabric background made from the two templates put together to form one template.

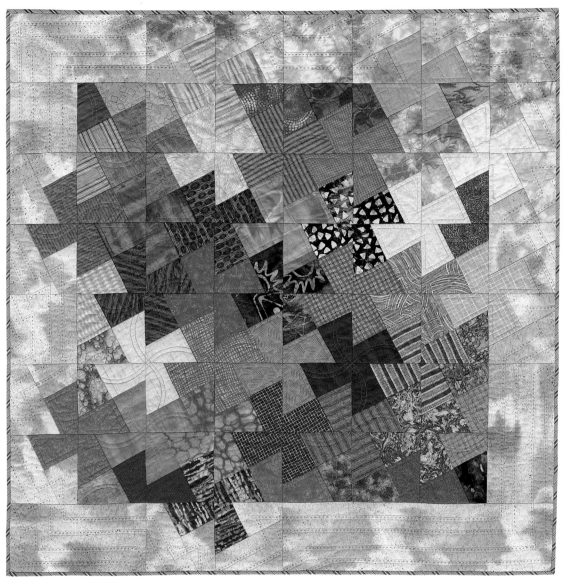

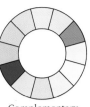

Complementary

Orange and Blue Pinwheels. 46½" x 46½". 2002. Mary Mashuta.

ORANGE AND BLUE PINWHEELS

This was the first quilt I made using the Pinwheel block, although it took me forever to get around to quilting it. The layout is very obvious, but within the narrow scheme, there is quite a variety of fabric types. The "sky" fabric border with extended Pinwheels adds whimsy and lightens the piece.

Rule #1: Color = complements of orange and blue

Rule #2: Block layout = alternate orange and blue

Rule #3: Fabrics = wide variety of printed solids + hand-dye look-alikes + batiks + stripes + subtle plaids + dots

Rule #4: Border = sky fabric

Rule #5: Border = a few floating Pinwheels extend into border

DESIGN HINTS
- If you run out of fabric you can substitute something similar, as I did in the upper right border.
- A bias-cut stripe binding pulls the viewer's eye around the quilt.
- You can embellish machine quilting with hand-stitched perle cotton.

Kailua-Kona Escape. 46"x 46". 1999. Becky Keck, Martinez, California. Quilted by New Pieces, Berkeley, California

KAILUA-KONA ESCAPE AND SUNSHINE AND WINDMILLS

Becky Keck started with the complements of red-orange and blue-green, but turned her colors into extended complements. Since you look to both sides of your complementary colors to get this scheme, you get to work with six colors instead of two. The two groupings of colors are opposite each other, but it isn't so obvious and contrived as the traditional complements.

Becky and Karen Dugas used a similar range of pattern types, but Karen favored a different palette. She began with yellow-orange and blue-violet and created extended complements just like Becky did with the adjoining colors. It's fun to see how starting in different spots on the color wheel can produce such different results. Both quilters found it helpful to have a large collection of fabric that includes a variety of pattern, as well as color and value.

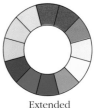

Extended
Complementary

Sunshine and Windmills. 46½" x 46". 1999. Karen Dugas, Pleasant Hill, California.
Quilted by New Pieces, Berkeley, California.

Rule #1: Color = extended comple-
    ments: Becky used red/
    red-orange/ orange and
    blue/blue-green/yellow-
    green and Karen used
    orange/yellow-orange/
    yellow and blue/blue-
    violet/violet

Rule #2: Block layout = random
    to edge

Rule #3: Fabrics = batiks, stripes,
    wispy solids, dots

Rule #4: Border = none, blocks
    to edge

DESIGN HINT
• Keep the eye of the viewer
  moving by randomly repeating a color throughout the
  quilt. Pick any color to see
  this working in Becky and
  Karen's quilts.

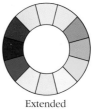

Extended
Complementary

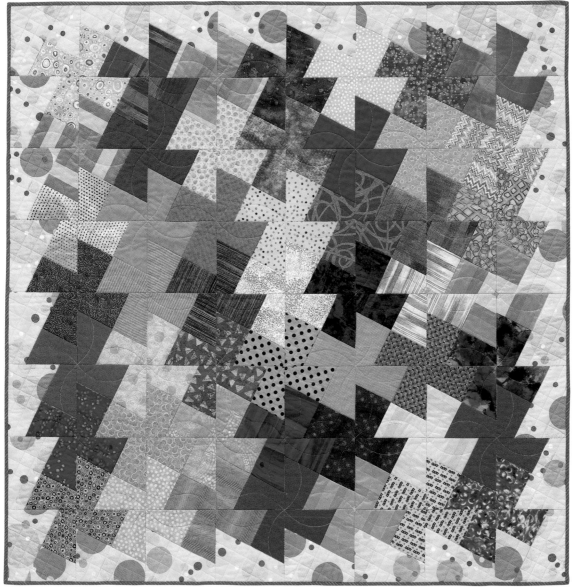

Triad Pinwheel. 47" x 47". 2002. Mary Mashuta.

TRIAD PINWHEEL

I decided to see what I could do with a triad color scheme. I picked secondary colors rather than the primary ones.

I had previously extended a few triangles into the border, but it dawned on me that all the pinwheels could be completed and extended. This was my chance to show off a cheerful polka dot print! The new, completed triangles appear to float on the pieced one-fabric background.

Rule #1: Color = triad of red-violet/yellow-orange/blue-green

Rule #2: Block layout = random

Rule #3: Fabric = solids, stripes, dots, batiks, allover designs

Rule #4: Border = floats behind completed pinwheels

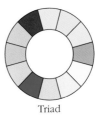

Triad

DESIGN HINTS

- The border is one of the zones where you can place a large-scale print.

- Using various sized prints raises the activity level.

- Template (page 93) used backward, so pinwheels appear to spin in the opposite direction.

The Altamont Pass. 50" x 50". 1998. Barbara Blessington, Sacramento, California

Sweet William. 42" x 49" top. 2000. Joann Cleckner, Petaluma, California.

Analogous

DESIGN HINTS
- The temperature change (page 10) between the neutral pinwheels allows you to see them as individual pinwheels.
- A few pinwheels extending into the border add playfulness.

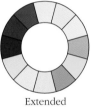

Extended Complementary

DESIGN HINT
- Four block corners made from different colors and fabrics raise the activity level.

THE ALTAMONT PASS

Barbara Blessington selected the colors for her quilt from a traditional border print that was an analogous scheme. Many quilters begin with a "focus" fabric and pull their colors from that. The quilt depicts the Altamont Pass in California where windmill farms generate electricity.

Rule #1: Color = analogous of peachy-pink, hot pink, dirty golds, and dirty greens; variety of warm and cool beiges

Rule #2: Block Layout = diagonal flow of dark to light

Rule #3: Fabrics = border print + bamboo print + batiks and other wispy solids + woven and printed plaids and stripes

Rule #4: Border = border print

Rule #5: Border = a few floating triangles extend into border

SWEET WILLIAM

Joann Cleckner thought it wouldn't be too hard to make a quilt with her favorite color, which is purple. When she realized that she would have to work with oranges and yellow-greens to have extended complements, she had to think again.

She ended up deciding to give it a go, and she hand-dyed fabric to supplement what was in her collection. The hand-dye-look, gold border is a perfect frame for her blocks.

Rule #1: Color = extended complements of yellow-orange/ yellow/yellow-green and blue-violet/violet/red/violet

Rule #2: Block layout = random

Rule #3: Fabric = subtle allover prints + hand-dyes

Rule #4: Border = traditional unpieced border with block corners

Rule #5: Border = a few floating pinwheels extend into border

Randomly arranged block prints from India.

Two colorway stripe + gradation of hand-dyed fabric.

Polychromatic

Off-the-Shelf Stripes. 2001. Mary Mashuta. Created for "Renaissance, the 2001 Bernina Fashion Show." Modeled by Elsa Rosborough. Photo by Perrault Studios.

OFF-THE-SHELF STRIPES

I like to make quilted jackets and coats with allover pieced designs. I find repeating the blocks pieced in stripes a sophisticated look for national runway shows, where graphics are important. "Across the crowded room" viewing is standard. This set of six stripes was purchased in the New York Garment District.

Rule #1: Color = polychromatic

Rule #2: Block layout = arrange stripes by row

Rule #3: Block layout = alternate stripes with randomly placed solids

Rule #4: Fabrics = for entire ensemble, two colorways of three stripes + denim weave solid cottons

Here are two other Pinwheel samples that would be perfect for garments. Pieced garments can be subtle and sophisticated. They don't have to make as strong a statement as runway garments do.

Using a simple, one-template block such as Pinwheel allows you to concentrate on color, fabric, and design rather than complicated piecing. You'll even have time and energy to come up with an interesting border.

DESIGN HINTS
- Pieced garments are smaller scale than quilts. Consider the size of your blocks. Jackets and coats can take larger blocks than vests.
- Place darker solids in the bottom half-row of pinwheels to define the jacket edge.

CHAPTER SEVEN

Double Star

I added a second diagonal line to the units of Naoko Star (pages 21 and 30) and came up with Double Star. Now I have a tessellation like the Pinwheel and Windmill blocks. New stars form when four adjoining same-color triangles touch. There are still only two pattern templates to deal with, a skinny right-angle triangle and a parallelogram. You need two triangles and one parallelogram for each unit.

Rule #1: Stars = bright fabrics

Rule #2: Parallelograms = car fabric from Mary's Driver's Ed Collection

Car Stars. Giny Dixon and Mary Mashuta.

Note: It is very important to cut all the fabric right side up. Absolutely do not fold your fabric during cutting. Fabric can be stacked, but make sure each fabric is right side up in the stack. Mark the "right" side of your template.

DOUBLE STAR VARIABLES

Double Star has two variables, or zones, for fabric placement. Let's look at two ways of coloring the same block. In *Car Stars*, the stars have to hold their own against a busy, figurative background so they are crayon-box-bright.

In *Twinkling Stars*, the emphasis changes to the background, or second variable, because all the stars have been cut from the same print.

Rule #1: Stars = all from same print

Rule #2: Parallelograms = variety of blues randomly placed

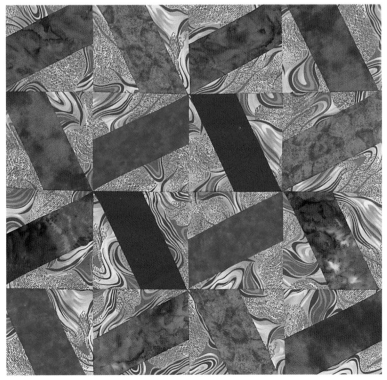

Twinkling Stars. Giny Dixon.

Twist and Twinkle.
58½" x 58½". 2001.
Rita Young Kilstrom.
Arnold, California.

TWIST AND TWINKLE

Rita Kilstrom turned her complements of orange and blue into extended complements because more fabrics make for a more visually interesting quilt.

Muted pattern prints aren't discernable until mid-viewing distance. Then we come closer to see the prints even better and are drawn into the quilt without realizing it. Rita floated her stars on a symmetrical dark-and-light border rather than running them to the edge.

Rule #1: Color = extended complements of red-orange/ orange/yellow-orange and blue-violet/blue/ blue-green

Rule #2: Stars = 32 different fabrics from the orange side of the color wheel

Rule #3: Parallelograms = variety of blues, some repeated

Rule #4: Fabrics = patterned fabrics, mostly limited to muted patterns with little value contrast

Rule #5: Border = symmetrical with dark corners

Extended
Complementary

DESIGN HINTS
• An accent cording using the complement makes the color at the edge of the quilt "pop."

• For a floating effect, Rita added an extra 2" strip to the outside blue blocks.

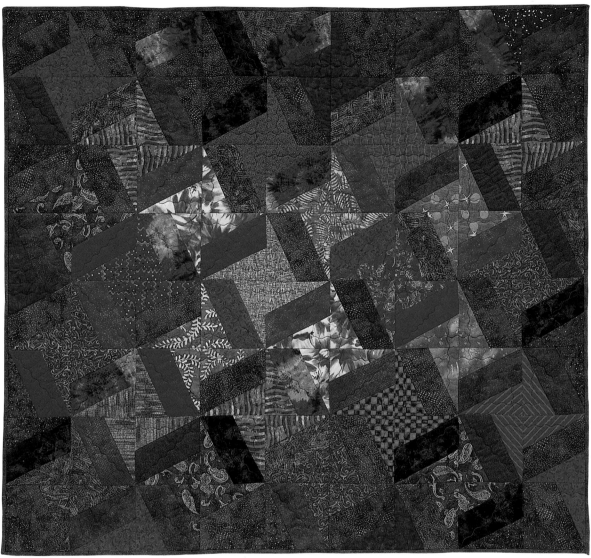

Starry Night. 52½" x 47". 2002. Giny Dixon, Danville, California.

STARRY NIGHT

Giny Dixon's concept was to have recognizable stars in the middle of her quilt and work toward darker, barely discernable stars, which would melt into the background by the time she reached the edge.

Giny wanted a quilt that was mostly dark with only a few light highlights. She picked a darkened triad color scheme, with a lot of blue, some red, and a dash of yellow. The quilt is mysterious and draws us in to see it at a closer distance.

Rule #1: Color = triad of red, blue, and yellow

Rule #2: Stars = random colors with darker at edge

Rule #3: Parallelograms = random blues

Rule #4: Fabric = geometrics + wispy prints and printed solids

Rule #5: Border = none, but darker stars at edge create an the illusion of one

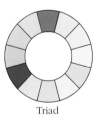

Triad

DESIGN HINTS
- The colors of your scheme don't have to be used in equal amounts.
- In more sophisticated quilts, the proportions of light, medium, and dark are not necessarily equal.

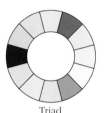

Triad

Triad Stars. 48" x 59½". 2002. Mary Mashuta. Quilted by Barbara Wilson, Citrus Heights, California.

DESIGN HINTS

- After everything is in place, fine-tune by looking at one area at a time. Look at the stars; look at the background.
- Purchased fabric will never have the perfect gradations you can get with hand-dyes. Imperfection can make a livelier quilt.

TRIAD STARS

Most of us don't like all colors equally. Periwinkle/blue-violet, was a color I didn't like so I purposely picked a triad color scheme that included it, and collected fabrics for a year.

Rita and Giny had arranged their blues randomly so I decided to be more orderly in placing mine. All the stars couldn't have their own personal background because Double Star is a continuous pattern.

The leftover, intermediary yellow-green stars end up with mixed backgrounds. Also, notice how I played with value in arranging the stars and backgrounds.

Rule #1: Color = triad of red-orange/yellow-green/blue-violet

Rule #2: Stars = alternate rows of orange-red and yellow-green

Rule #3: Parallelograms = periwinkle

Rule #4: Fabrics = stripes, dots, and printed solids. Most muted with low contrast.

Rule #5: Layout = stars light to dark beginning at top; background parallelograms dark at top to light at bottom

Rule #6: Border = none, blocks to edge

Alaskan Stars. 82" x 94". 2002. George Taylor, Anchorage, Alaska

ALASKAN STARS

George Taylor knew I liked using collections. He had three sets of fabric in many colorways. George's stripes are multicolor but the end result is always muted because the colors are grayed. There is also an absence of white. Subtle can be very good.

Even though there are three different patterns, George's dots have a consistent feel because they are all two-color prints with about the same size dots.

Rule #1: Color = polychromatic

Rule #2: Stars = random mix of woven stripes and dots

Rule #3: Parallelograms = hand-dyed-look solids

Rule #4: Border = none, blocks to edge

Polychromatic

DESIGN HINT
- Printed solids with a streaky look have more action in them so they raise the activity level. (Your eyes rest longer on plain solids.)

Feed Sack Stars. 53½" x 53½". 2002. Mary Mashuta.

FEED SACK STARS

I have a sizable feed sack collection. Most of them are loosely woven, so simple blocks work best. Making two similar quilts gave me the opportunity to experiment.

In *Feed Sack Stars*, my stripes had to hold their own against the busy, orange-and-white paisley background. Darker stripes with less white worked, but paler ones with a lot of white didn't because they blended. I worked a couple

of lighter stars in, but only after I moved a lot of pieces around on the design wall.

Rule #1: Color = analogous, orange to blue-green

Rule #2: Stars = stripes

Rule #3: Parallelograms = orange and white paisley

Rule #4: Fabrics = feed sack stripes + feed sack paisley

Rule #5: Border = four plaids + four plaid corners

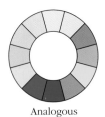

Analogous

DESIGN HINT

• A multifabric border raises the activity level of the whole quilt.

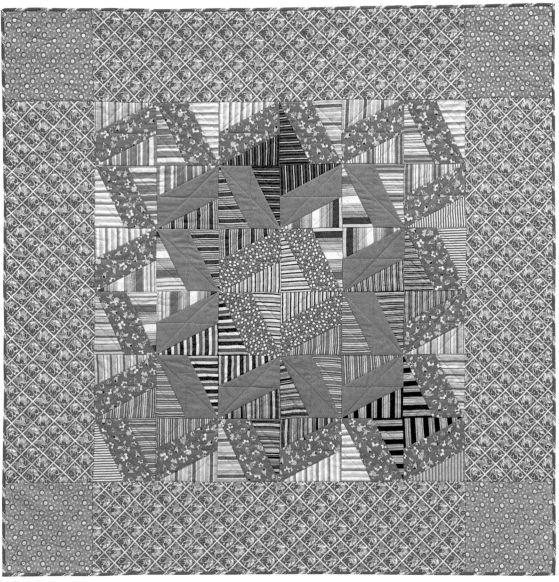

More Feed Sack Stars. 53½" x 53½". 2002. Mary Mashuta.

MORE FEED SACK STARS

There wasn't enough fabric to cut all the background parallelograms I needed, so making-do was a necessity. My fabrics were too different for a random mix, so arranging the three in concentric circles worked best.

I used many of the same darker stripe stars that I had in the first quilt, but I managed to tuck pale-stripe half-stars around the edge.

Rule #1: Color = analogous, orange to blue-green, again

Rule #2: Stars = stripes, again

Rule #3: Parallelograms = concentric circles of three blue-green fabrics

Rule #4: Fabrics = feed sack stripes + feed sack prints + feed sack solid

Rule #5: Border = traditional same-fabric sides + same-fabric corners

DESIGN HINT
• Limiting the number of fabrics in the border treatment helps calm down the activity level of the center of the quilt.

A quilt is never done until it's done. One design choice affects the next.

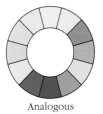

Analogous

CHAPTER EIGHT

Triple Pinwheel

Triple Pinwheel is
an allover design.
The idea is to make
sure you can see
all the pinwheels.

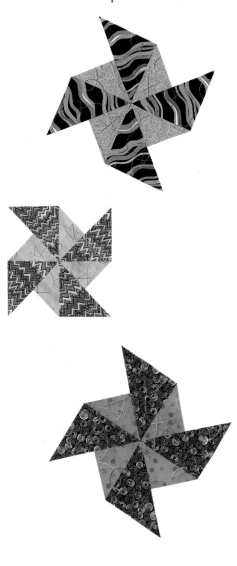

Triple Pinwheel is quite different from the traditional Pinwheel previously discussed. The block is made up of two sizes of right angle triangles that each form pinwheels. I call this block a Triple Pinwheel, but it is also called Whirligig, Windmill, or Whirling Windmill. There are leftover triangles in the corners of the block after the large and small pinwheels are colored. These are usually considered the negative space. Not many people pay any attention to them, but I do.

Since I am looking for tessellations, I realized the corner triangles could be the beginning of new pinwheels if they connected with same-fabric triangles in adjoining blocks. Triple Pinwheel is another example of "how you see it is not how you sew it." (It is sewn as units rather than blocks.)

Triple Pinwheel is an allover design. The idea is to make sure you can see all the pinwheels. To accomplish this you have to change color, value, and/or pattern just as you do in the basic Pinwheel quilts.

Usually a specific color is chosen for the large triangles, but to keep things more interesting, a variety of same-color fabrics are selected. After the large triangles are moved around and placed, the small triangles are positioned. It is important to keep the eye moving by repeating colors randomly throughout the quilt. Notice how the eight yellow pinwheels are placed in *New Year's at the Palladion*.

The quilt can be borderless, but it is clunky. You can create an optical border by adding another half row of blocks around the completed blocks. The secondary small pinwheels become completed and they contrast against fabric that is somehow different from what is in the quilt center.

NEW YEAR'S AT THE PALLADION

Crayon-box-bright colors add festivity to a New Year's Collection. Notice the one eye-catching zigzag stripe that is used in four large pinwheels, and again, in three small ones. This is the only exception to my rule: If the fabric appears in the large triangles, it doesn't repeat in the smaller ones. Rules can be occasionally broken, but must be followed the majority of the time.

Rule #1: Color = polychromatic

Rule #2: Large Pinwheels = black-background fabrics

Rule #3: Small Pinwheels = multicolored fabrics

Rule #4: Fabric = festive and happy nighttime fabrics
feature streamers, fireworks, and stars. To fill in,
lots of playful dots and whimsical stripes from other collections

Rule #5: Border = streamer fabric + fill-ins arranged in a sequence rather
than randomly

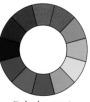

Polychromatic

DESIGN HINTS
- When you run out of border fabric, determine the activity level of the quilt before you find a solution for placing the additional fabrics.
- A straight-cut stripe binding contains activity at the edge.

New Year's at the Palladion. 59" x 68". 2000. Mary Mashuta.
Quilted at New Pieces, Berkeley, California.

Blueberry Pie.
67" x 68". 2002.
Karen Dugas.
Pleasant Hill, California.
Quilted by New Pieces,
Berkeley, California.

BLUEBERRY PIE

Karen Dugas decided to use lots of large-scale prints and see what would happen. Some pinwheels show; some disappear, just like blocks do in many scrap quilts.

She used two colors in the large pinwheels. She accentuated the color change of her two-color borders by placing opposite-color large pinwheels next to each border. This is subtle; you don't get it at first.

Rule #1: Color = triad of red-orange/yellow-green/blue-violet

Rule #2: Large pinwheels = yellow-green and blue-violet

Rule #3: Small pinwheels = above + red-orange

Rule #4: Fabric = assorted, but lots of large scale prints

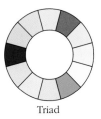

Triad

DESIGN HINT
• Be open to trying new things. You'll be delighted when you make it work.

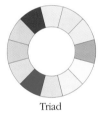

Triad

Raspberry Swirl.
80" x 89½". 2002.
Becky Keck, Martinez,
California. Quilted by
New Pieces, Berkeley,
California.

RASPBERRY SWIRL

Becky Keck began with a triad color scheme when she started selecting fabrics from her collection. Her fabrics more or less fit into the scheme, but she wasn't rigid and strayed from time to time.

Becky Keck's large pinwheels are always from the same color range so the backbone of the quilt is created even though there is tremendous variety from block to block. Five repetitions of the large-scale "hippy-looking" print work in the large quilt. It would be hard to hide a print like this in a smaller quilt because one or two blocks would call too much attention to themselves.

Rule #1: Color = triad of yellow orange/ blue-green/red-violet

Rule #2: Big pinwheels = red-violet

Rule #3: Small pinwheels = yellow-orange + blue-green

Rule #4: Border = raspberry dot print

DESIGN HINTS
- Using an extra two-inch same-fabric strip at the quilt edge makes the border triangles float a little bit more.
- The same-fabric two-inch strip is also a "fudge-factor" when it comes time to square-up your quilt.
- The densely patterned contemporary dot fabric helps to contain the frenzy of the quilt center.

Pickle Dish. 39½" x 39½". 2002.
Mary Mashuta and Rebecca
Rohrkaste, Berkeley, California.
Quilted by Rebecca Rohrkaste.

PICKLE DISH

I combined several pushed-neutral kits and tried to create extended complements. Rebecca Rohrkaste and I tried to compose the quilt. We couldn't quite fit in the brightest gold pinwheels until Rebecca volunteered a dirty gold from her own private stash. It acted as an intermediary between gold and green.

Rule #1: Color = extended complements of violet/red-violet/ but no blue-violet. On the other side of the color wheel, dirty shades of yellow-orange/yellow/yellow-green

Rule #2: Large pinwheels = violet and red/violet

Rule #3: Small pinwheels = yellow-green/yellow/yellow-orange

Rule #4: Fabric = solids

Rule #5: Border = printed solid prints

Extended
Complementary

DESIGN HINTS

• When a color stands out too much, don't take it out. Instead, see if you can find an intermediary fabric to bridge the gap between it and the colors or values closest to it.

• When you run out of border fabric, experiment.

CHRISTMAS PINWHEELS

The palette of Christmas colors is pretty limited. Buy any colors that are different so you can have more variety.

I paid attention to the busy prints that contained white and made sure they weren't clustered, but evenly distributed to keep the eye moving. I used three metallic-gold scraps to piece the border.

Rule #1: Color = complements of red and green

Rule #2: Large pinwheels = all green

Rule #3: Small pinwheels = both red and green

Rule #4: Fabrics = Christmas prints + assorted red and/or green stripes

Rule #5: Border = metallic gold

Christmas Pinwheels. 39½" x39½". 2002. Mary Mashuta.
Quilted by Barbara Wilson, Citrus Heights, California.

Complementary

DESIGN HINTS

• Stripes, plaids, dots, and wispy solids work well as fill-ins to extend your theme collection.

• Small-motif patterns tend to be spotty, particularly if the motifs are on a white background. Don't commit until you try moving them around.

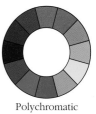

DESIGN HINT

- A few lighter-value pinwheels add sparkle and keep our eye moving around the quilt. They are randomly, yet strategically placed.

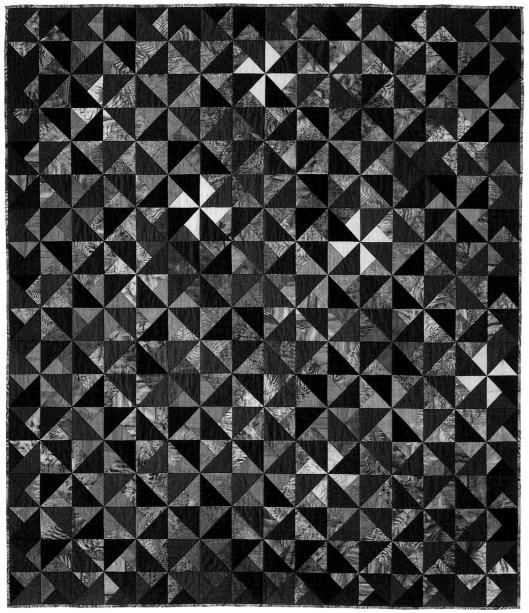

South African Pinwheels. 78" x 89". 2002. George Taylor, Anchorage, Alaska.

SOUTH AFRICAN PINWHEELS

George Taylor wanted to showcase a special collection of hand-dyed fabrics from South Africa. There were three distinct print types to add variety and visual interest; vegetable matter, wispy solids, and a black crackle over-dye.

George often disobeys my rules. He randomly placed greens in the large triangle pinwheels, and turned them into negative space. George showcased his collection of hand-dyed fabrics in the small pinwheels. He broke my rules and came up with his own set. Good for him!

Rule #1: Color = polychromatic

Rule #2: Large pinwheels = four greens randomly placed

Rule #3: Small pinwheels = three hand-dyed prints in many colors

Rule #4: Border = fill in with green so small pinwheels run to edge

The Pinwheel and Triple Pinwheel blocks both create allover pinwheel designs even though they have different-shaped templates. The same quilt rules can be applied to designing quilts with either block.

CHAPTER NINE

Circle within Circle

The traditional Circle within Circle block consists of a circle of eight joined wedges. I think of it as a donut appliquéd to a solid background, just as Dresden Plate is. I featured the block in *Cotton Candy Quilts*, but divided the background behind the ring into four squares. It became more interesting because I got to choose four negative-space colors rather than just one.

If the block is pieced rather than appliquéd, even more color choices are possible because four new fabrics can be placed in the center quarter-circles. For construction purposes, there are four separate units in the block. Often units, rather than complete blocks, make up the design as you will see in this chapter.

Circle within Circle block made with florals in each zone.

The pieced unit has three variables, or zones: the wedges that make up the ring, the inner quarter-circle, and a background corner piece. With all these choices, there are only three templates. The block is perfect to show off a fabric collection. Refer to page 36 to see *Stop, Look, and Listen*, which features Driver's Ed fabrics.

Once the Circle within Circle block is broken into quarter-circle units, it is possible to arrange the segments in many different ways and end up with a very contemporary looking quilt. This can be randomly worked out on a design wall, but most quilters find it easier to play with the layout on paper as a first step. Then you have a road map to follow when the actual pieces are placed on the design wall. (Remember, don't sew the blocks until everything is composed.)

Students taking my Buncha Dots class use the Circle within Circle block, so you will see lots of dots in the following pages.

Detail of *Rainbow Sprinkle Confections* (page 68), Pat Dicker.

BEACH COLORS

Giny Dixon wanted a rectangular quilt to hang in her dining room. She went for a traditional layout, but half-circles at the edge were more interesting than using all complete circles.

Giny limited herself to one fabric type, hand-dyes and hand-dye look-alikes. She had to rely on color and value changes to distinguish the block parts. The ring design comes in and out of focus, we are drawn into the quilt.

Rule #1: Color = Polychromatic

Rule #2: Wedges = mostly-solid magenta, green, blue, and purple

Rule #3: Quarter-circles = match corners

Rule #4: Corners = streaky polychromatic, but mainly blue

Rule #5: Fabric = hand-dyes + hand-dye look-alikes

Rule #6: Format = full circles with half circles at edge

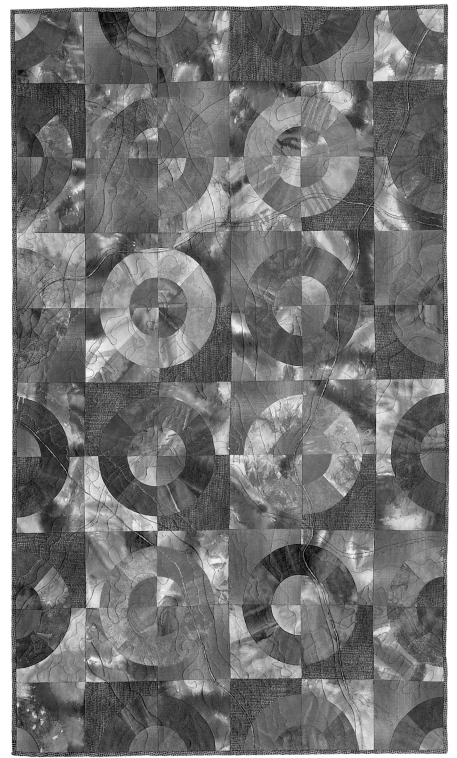

Beach Colors. 37" x 60½". 2002. Giny Dixon, Danville, California

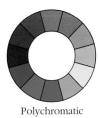

Polychromatic

DESIGN HINT
• When using fabrics that are generally alike, make sure there is enough contrast between individual pieces. Move pieces around to find the best location, if necessary.

Rainbow Sprinkle Confections. 50" x 62". 2002. Pat Dicker, Mill Valley, CA

Label, Pat Dicker.

Polychromatic

DESIGN HINTS
- If making multiple same-color rings, make sure none are exactly alike. Exact repetitions trap and stop the eye.
- Expand your idea of what a dot is. Pat used three cherry prints!

RAINBOW SPRINKLE CONFECTIONS

Pat Dicker had lots of bright dots for her quilt, however, she had to put some order in the chaos. She arranged her background colors diagonally, but nothing was holding the quilt together. Making all the background corners in the outside squares dark finally did it. She needed a "border" to contain all the busy fabrics.

Rule #1: Color = polychromatic

Rule #2: Wedges = eight one-color fabrics in each ring

Rule #3: Quarter-circles = match corner in color, but not in fabric

Rule #4: Corners = match quarter-circle in color, but not in fabric

Rule #5: Fabric = dots

Rule #6: Format = straight-forward circles, but each of the four units has different fabrics

Rule #7: Border = outside blocks have black or dark blue backgrounds

Traveling in the Right Circles. 41½" x 36". 2001. Barbara Blessington, Sacramento, CA

TRAVELING IN THE RIGHT CIRCLES

Barbara Blessington used a glued mock-up of the blocks as a guide to place the fabric pieces. She purchased just the right fabric for her background. The squiggly, abstract print stays the same, only the color changes. Having all the background corner pieces the same pattern helps to calm the composition.

Rule #1: Color = polychromatic

Rule #2: Wedges = bright dots

Rule #3: Quarter-circles = hand-dyes and hand-dye look-alikes

Rule #4: Corners = five colorways squiggly abstract

Rule #5: Fabric = three categories by zone

Rule #6: Format = random, mostly three-quarter circles

The Circle within Circle block has only three templates, but there are many color and fabric choices to make. When planning a quilt with this block, it helps to concentrate on what you are doing in one zone at a time.

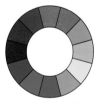

Polychromatic

DESIGN HINTS
- Grayed background fabrics are a perfect foil to contrast brighter fan wedges against.
- Using multiple colorways of one print in the background, rather than a lot of different prints, lowers the activity level.

Roundabout Dots. 60" x 60". 2000. Mary Mashuta.

ROUNDABOUT DOTS

I created *Roundabout Dots* for the Rod Buffington group show "Double Vision: Companions and Choices." He made a dot collage with my block, some of my dot fabrics, and dots he painted. The radiating quilt layout is based on a 1909 embroidered, velvet fan quilt. Following the cues given in the inspirational quilt, I knew what colors to place in each of the three zones.

Rule #1: Color = polychromatic

Rule #2: Wedges = any dots not in other two zones

Rule #3: Quarter-circles = dots with red background

Rule #4: Corners = dots with black background

Rule #5: Fabric = dots

Rule #6: Format = concentric rows from center

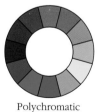

Polychromatic

DESIGN HINT
• Concentrate on one zone at a time so you don't get confused.

Dotty Arches. 49" x 49". 2001. Karen Dugas, Pleasant Hill, California. Quilted by New Pieces, Berkeley, California.

DOTTY ARCHES

Karen Dugas liked the ***Roundabout Dots*** layout. Her quilt has color but it's subtle rather than crayon-box-bright. The negative space beiges and grays vary in temperature and contrast against each other. Beiges stretch from sandy pink all the way over to gold. Warm taupe-grays stretch into blue-grays. Karen is another master of subtle color use.

Rule #1: Color = subtle polychromatic

Rule #2: Wedges = mostly neutral with a little color

Rule #3: Quarter-circles = beige and gray

Rule #4: Corners = beige and gray

Rule #5: Fabric = dots

Rule #6: Format = concentric rows from center.

Polychromatic

DESIGN HINT
- Arrange the subtle background in concentric rings of gray and beige to give more impact.

Dotty Color Wheel. 59" x 59". 2000. Karen Dugas, Pleasant Hill, California. Quilted by New Pieces, Berkeley, California.

DOTTY COLOR WHEEL

Karen Dugas ended up with a spectacular background for her quilt, but it took work. She had four colorways of a variegated plaid, but there was too much contrast between them to be subtle. She limited herself to the orange ones and substituted fern batiks in the orange-pink-purple range. There is a lot happening in the background, yet it isn't overwhelming.

Rule #1: Color = polychromatic

Rule #2: Wedges = single color dots per ring

Rule #3: Quarter-circles = single color dots per ring

Rule #4: Corners = orange, pink, and purple plaids and fern prints

Rule #5: Fabric = categories by zone

Rule #6: Format = mostly three-quarter circles with half circles at edge

Polychromatic

DESIGN HINT

• Deciding on a rule like limiting the wedges in each ring to only one color is one way to exercise control over many colors.

Dot. Dot. Dot. 62" x 61". 1999. Mary Mashuta.

DOT. DOT. DOT.

I came up with the serpentine layout by playing around with the pieces after they were randomly laid out on my design wall, but there was too much happening. I needed some order in the chaos.

I rearranged the background corners in each serpentine row by color. Then I balanced the value or color flow a little from dark to light or warm to cool.

Rule #1: Color = polychromatic

Rule #2: Wedges = random

Rule #3: Quarter-circles = random

Rule #4: Corners = one color flow for each serpentine row

Rule #5: Fabric = dots

Rule #6: Format = serpentine rows

Polychromatic

DESIGN HINT

• When you get all the pieces arranged on the wall, stand back and take a look, one zone at a time.

CHAPTER TEN

Serpentine Curves

What is exciting about Serpentine Curves is that the two units are involved in different color flows. This interlocking design is a good example of the whole being more than the sum of the parts.

Picket fence. Mendocino, California. Photo by author.

I wanted a block where the design could flow from unit to unit, block to block. In looking at other curved blocks, I discovered the secret to making this happen is to have the curve start at the mid-point of the side seams. (When you serpentine Circle within Circle units, for example, this doesn't happen. See *Dot. Dot. Dot.* on page 73) The visual design is created when same-fabric and similar-color pieces flow into each other, sometimes turning corners.

Serpentine Curves has two templates so there are only two variables. Two units make up a block and the diagonal seam where they are stitched together reinforces the two curves of the units. Structurally and visually you have a good start on diagonal emphasis. Repetitive fabric and color placement does the trick!

What is exciting about Serpentine Curves is that the two units are involved in different color flows. This interlocking design is a good example of the whole being more than the sum of the parts.

I like stripes, I like chevrons, and I like striped chevrons. The repetitive lines are just like looking at a picket fence. Before you know it, your eyes have turned the corner.

We use Serpentine Curves in my Stripes Go Contemporary Class so you will see lots of stripes in this chapter. At the end of the chapter, Julie Anderson proves you don't have to use stripes.

SALMON RUN

Pat Hastings's stripes look fairly traditional until you look carefully and discover that traditional small-scale stripes are more exciting then they used to be. The straight lines are slightly curvy; many look like they were drawn freehand with markers rather than with a pen and ruler. Some are streaky because of the strong influence of hand-dyed fabrics. Notice how effective the coral batik is when cut as a stripe.

Pat resorted to using the wrong side of some of the fabrics when they looked too bright, or just to add value variety.

Rule #1: Color = polychromatic, but lots in the blue and orange range

Rule #2: Polygon = soft color rows + more contrasting rows

Rule #3: Quarter-circle = analogous flows in yellow to orange range + mixed colors for quarter center circles

Rule #4: Fabric = variety of stripes, batiks, solids, printed solids, plaids

Rule #5: Format = linear serpentine rows

Salmon Run. 28" x 42". 2002. Pat B. Hastings, Stevensville, Montana.

Polychromatic

DESIGN HINT
• You don't always have to make big quilts, Just make sure your small quilts say enough.

Trumpet Vine. 59" x 59" 1997. Mary Mashuta.

TRUMPET VINE

Two tries at making a quilt called ***Vegetable Medley***, failed. Out went four colorways of a busy stripe and the vegetables! You won't believe how easily what remained went together. To my amazement, when I looked out my studio window I saw the trumpet vine and realized it contained the colors in my quilt! Making quilts is a lot like life. We don't always get what we want, sometimes it's actually better.

Rule #1: Color = Variety up close, but basically analogous

Rule #2: Polygon = repeat fabric and color in flows

Rule #3: Quarter-circle = repeat fabric or similar fabric in flows

Rule #4: Fabric = woven and printed stripes + one beautiful hand-dyed stripe by Stacy Michell + hand-dyes + a few printed and wispy solids

Rule #5: Format = serpentine in diagonal rows

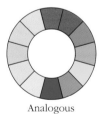

Analogous

DESIGN HINTS

- Repetition is the key to the success of this design.
- Don't sew when you're frustrated, you won't want to rip stitches and make necessary changes later.

Mixed Greens. 57" x 57". 1998. Mary Mashuta.

MIXED GREENS

I made a quilt for the Women of Taste show, which paired me with Annie Somerville, the Executive Chef of my favorite vegetarian restaurant. Greens has views of the San Francisco Marina and the Golden Gate Bridge.

Annie got employees to trace their hands for me to use in the quilt. My recycled stash of stripes and vegetables from *Trumpet Vine* were perfect. As Annie said, "You don't always have to start from scratch."

Rule #1: Color = almost polychromatic

Rule #2: Polygons = contrast of prints or prints and stripes

Rule #3: Quarter-circle = vegetables + assorted prints + wispy solids

Rule #4: Whole-circle border = clouds + yellows

Rule #5: Hand border = green hands + large triangles filled with mostly-green stripes

Rule #6: Fabric = stripes + vegetable prints + cloud prints + assorted low contrast prints and printed solids

Rule #7: Format = Blocks on-square surrounded by two borders

Polychromatic

DESIGN HINTS

- When the blocks aren't sewn together, it is easy to slightly alter the placement of the fabrics and not have to rip a stitch.
- Clouds need to be cut right side up.

A Few Days in Provence. 62" x 62". 1998. Mary Mashuta.

A FEW DAYS IN PROVENCE

After visiting Provence, I wanted to capture in a quilt how the incredible light enhanced everything. I also wanted to showcase the small-scale prints that are synonymous with the region and purchased fabrics in expensive showrooms and at an open market in Arles. They were a wonderful example of high-end design and inexpensively produced knock-offs. I wanted to include them all.

Rule #1: Color = tremendous variety up close, but basically triad

Rule #2: Polygon = repeated pattern or color in flows

Rule #3: Quarter-circle = repeated colors in flows, even though fabric and value may change slightly from unit to unit

Rule #4: Fabrics = wide assortment of printed and woven stripes + Provençal prints + clouds + hand-dyes + wispy solids

Rule #5: Format = serpentine in diagonal rows

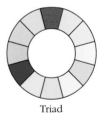

Triad

DESIGN HINTS

- A wide assortment of stripes keeps the viewer interested.
- Value contrast is important between the rows or everything blends together.
- The cloud fabrics add whimsy to the quilt.

Beach Daze. 55" x 54 ½". 2002. Becky Keck, Pleasant Hill, California.

BEACH DAZE

Becky Keck's set of stripes reminded her of beach umbrellas so she filled out the theme with cloud and bubbly dot fabrics. She knew to purchase multiple colorways of any fabrics that she could find.

As an added bonus, Becky figured out she could create an optical border while still using the Serpentine Curves block by contrasting dark and light value fabrics.

Rule #1: Color = polychromatic

Rule #2: Polygons = stripes

Rule #3: Quarter-circles = clouds in center + dots in border

Rule #4: Fabrics = stripes + clouds + bubbly dots

Rule #5: Format = diagonal serpentine in center + darker border

DESIGN HINTS

- Changing colorways, yet keeping the pattern constant, is a subtle way to give the viewer more to see, while still tying the quilt together through repetition of pattern.

- Often when we think we are using color to distinguish different parts of the block or quilt, what we are really using is value.

Polychromatic

Palancar Gardens. 56" x 49". 1999. Becky Keck, Martinez, California.

PALANCAR GARDENS

Becky Keck likes to go on scuba diving vacations with her husband. She wanted to create the underwater world of shifting lights, colors, coral, and fish.

Becky is a master at using batik fabrics and realized some could be cut as you would stripes. What you need is more-or-less straight lines that are more-or-less parallel to each other.

Rule #1: Color = polychromatic

Rule #2: Polygon = repeated flows of color and fabrics

Rule #3: Quarter-circle = bubbles and water

Rule #4: Fabrics = stripes + wide variety of batik cut as stripes + other underwater-look fabrics

Rule #5: Format = serpentine in diagonal rows

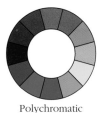

Polychromatic

DESIGN HINTS

- If you think a fabric could be cut to look like a stripe, but you're not sure, make a viewing window with your hands to mask the fabric and just look at a small rectangular or triangular portion.
- Expand your search for stripes to "striped" batiks for a softer look.

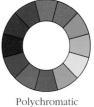

Polychromatic

- Fill out a collection of paisley fabrics with other prints that have a similar feel.
- Two color dots lower the activity level, multicolored dots raise the activity level.

Asian Fusion. 49" x 49½". 2002. Julie Anderson, Palo Alto, California.

ASIAN FUSION

Julie Anderson wanted to use paisleys rather than stripes. To highlight the zigzag patterns she was creating, Julie resorted to using two kinds of contrast. Complementary colors often bounce off each other in the sewing units. Value contrasts of dark against light also make for a bolder visual pattern. To make the zigzag work, she found she had to contrast two lighter lines against two darker lines to make it bold.

Rule #1: Color = polychromatic

Rule #2: Polygons = mostly paisleys

Rule #3: Quarter-circles = mostly dots

Rule #4: Fabric = paisley + supporting prints + dots

Rule #5: Format = serpentine in vertical linear rows with high contrast between every two rows

Serpentine Curves is a "less is more" kind of block. It has two templates and two zones to consider. It's a great block to show off several fabric collections at once, to learn how to make a color flow, and to learn how to make bold and supportive areas work together. This allover design is a good example of the whole being more than the sum of its parts.

CHAPTER ELEVEN

Air Ship Propeller

Detail of *Air Ship Propeller, II*. 1999. Barbara J. Wilson, Citrus Heights, California. Quilted by Dee Davis. Collection of Jan Fairbanks.

I was introduced to the Air Ship Propeller block when I was working on *Cotton Candy Quilts*. Barbara Wilson made a reproduction of her mom's quilt using feed sacks, just like her mom had done.

I persuaded Barbara to make a second quilt, but change the background colors from block to block. See how your perception of the pattern changes with this one change. *Air Ship Propeller, II* is all about the propellers while the abrupt color changes in *New Hot Wheels* makes you very aware of individual blocks.

I knew even more could be done with the block, but didn't pursue it until after *Cotton Candy Quilts* had gone to press. The 30s block could be given new life through the eyes of contemporary quilters. I realized that the block had five variables, or zones, that could operate independently of each other.

Three elements make up the positive space in the Air Ship Propeller block: propellers, propeller rings, and the centers.

Traditionally the propeller blades are the same fabric in a block, but different fabrics in other blocks. (They could also be done in a scrap-bag fashion and all be different.) Both prints and geometrics work.

A block has matching propeller rings, but they can change from block to block. Solid colors make the rings easy to distinguish from the print or geometric propellers.

The center circles match the rings in the block or are one color throughout the quilt.

The traditional negative space is created when the four corners join with the four large triangular pieces between them. However, if you look hard at *Air Ship Propeller, II* you will notice that the large triangle pieces could also form propellers!

The triangles become positive space when they are cut from contrasting rather than matching, background fabric. The fabric change makes them stand out rather than recede.

Detail of *New Hot Wheels*. 50" x 70". 1999. Barbara J. Wilson, Citrus Heights, California. Collection of Roberta Horton and Mary Mashuta.

DESIGN HINT
• Selecting one color for the circles and/or rings is a way of making a polychromatic quilt match your room.

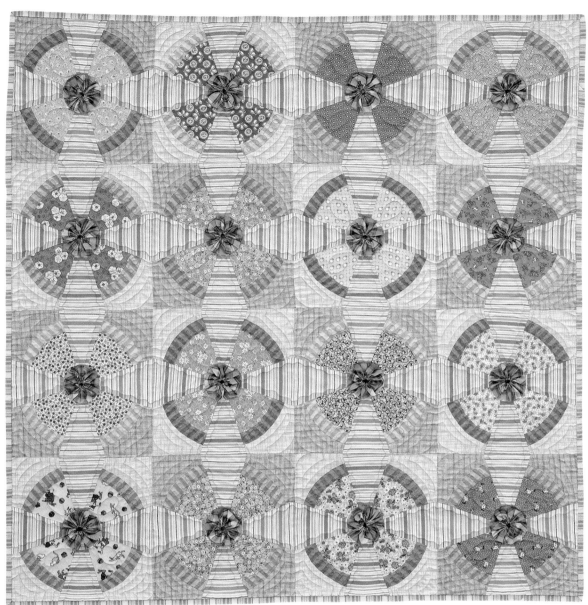

Repro Propellers. 39" x 38". 2002. Patricia Deforce, Oakland, California. Quilted by Kari Ruedisale, Lansing, Michigan.

REPRO PROPELLERS

Patricia Deforce discovered she could take a collection of 1930s prints and a two-colorway stripe in new directions. She was able to emphasize her high-contrast stripe, but still support it with a more subtle, low-contrast stripe. She also found two plaids to alternate in the background. The final detail, multicolored yoyos added a perfect 30s touch.

Rule #1: Color = polychromatic

Rule #2: Small propellers = 30s prints, one print per block

Rule #3: Rings = collection of 6 two-color stripes, one colorway per block

Rule #4: Corners = pink printed and pink woven plaids alternating by block

Rule #5: Large propellers = two colorways one stripe, alternated

Rule #6: Centers = plaid yoyos

Polychromatic

DESIGN HINT
• Cut the propeller stripes perpendicular to the length of the blades (the short distance) so they radiate out from the center of the block. This gives more movement than cutting them the long direction.

Serendipity Dots. 56" x 56". 2002. Mary Mashuta.

SERENDIPITY DOTS

I had fun composing blocks from my dot collection. One day Karen Dugas showed me a 1950s fashion fabric that she knew I would just have to have. They were made for each other. Talk about serendipity. I used two similar-but-different stripes for the large propellers because I ran out of fabric, but this gives you something to discover up close.

Rule #1: Color = polychromatic

Rule #2: Small propellers = dots, one print per block

Rule #3: Rings = 30s solids

Rule #4: Corners = wispy solids, randomly placed

Rule #5: Large propellers = two stripes, alternating

Rule #6: Centers = red gingham yoyos

Rule #7: Inner border = pink + darker pink plaid cornerstones with aqua gingham yoyos

Rule #8: Outer border = 50s fashion print + Propeller block corners

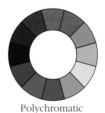

Polychromatic

DESIGN HINTS
• Multiple backgrounds can be subtle, the colors don't have to be high contrast.
• Be willing to try changes. Quilters are visual people. Don't just wonder about it in your head, try it!

Paisley Propellers. 63" x 63". 2002. Mary Mashuta.

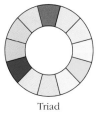

Triad

DESIGN HINTS

- When you're placing fabrics randomly, make sure that repeats aren't too close to each other, as very close repetition stops the eye.
- Throw in something unexpected, like the corner block stripe which I chose intuitively. It is your gift to the viewer for really looking at your quilt.
- Every design decision affects something else in the quilt.

PAISLEY PROPELLERS

I love paisley prints and keep adding them to my fabric collection. Some years they're beautiful and some they're so ugly I can barely bring myself to buy them. I hadn't tried a scrap quilt effect yet so I decided to mix the paisleys in each block. I knew the wonderful yellow border fabric was perfect the moment I saw it. Lucky me, I got to use it.

Rule #1: Color = triad of pink, yellow, blue

Rule #2: Small propellers = random paisleys, like scrap quilt

Rule #3: Rings = large variety of yellows

Rule #4: Corners = four pastel polychromatic dots

Rule #5: Large propellers = two pink stripes

Rule #6: Centers = two-value pink dot

Rule #7: Inner border = pink paisley from Provence + yellow corners

Rule #8: Outer border = yellow, French nineteenth-century reproduction floral + stripe + dot corners

New Propellers. 30" x 30". 2002. Barbara J. Wilson, Citrus Heights, California.

NEW PROPELLERS

Barbara Wilson's third quilt was like a doodle where she simply tried out ideas. She forgot the standard rules. The most consistent thing she used was blue-green propeller rings in all the blocks. This strong, circular repeated element pulls the individual blocks together. She opted to use a number of blue-greens, however.

Barbara's little quilt presents many design options to us. When a small propeller and its corners are cut from the same fabric they turn into a bigger propeller. Barbara decided to always make the four new propellers from different fabric within a block.

She also played around a lot with the original triangular negative space that wasn't negative space anymore. See how many different ways Barbara cut the stripe fabrics? You will probably find you prefer some better than others. Notice how the patched, stripe circles look almost three-dimensional.

Barbara's quilt encourages us to be more playful.

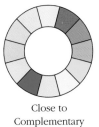

Close to
Complementary

DESIGN HINT
- Using slightly different blue-greens livens up the rings. The slight changes add to the playfulness of the quilt and raise the activity level.

Journey to the Back of Beyond. 39½" x 39½". 2002. Mary Mashuta.

JOURNEY TO THE BACK OF BEYOND

I was given leftover scraps from an Australian Aboriginal silk screen printing project. I borrowed Barbara Wilson's idea of placing the same fabric in the small propellers and corner pieces. Not only do my students learn from me, I learn from them.

I decided to think outside the box and run the propeller prints in diagonal lines from block to block. Each block has two prints: one runs diagonally to the left, the other runs diagonally to the right.

Rule #1: Almost polychromatic

Rule #2: Small propellers + corners = two sets of fabric placed diagonally across quilt

Rule #3: Rings = various rusts

Rule #4: Large propellers = Australian stripe + Indian stripe at border

Rule #5: Centers = Aboriginal red print + American red print at border

Almost Polychromatic

DESIGN HINTS
- Running the prints diagonally from block to block will help to put some order in the chaos of busy prints.
- Learn to think outside the box. You might be amazed with what you discover.

Spectrum Flight. 50" x 50". 2002. Julie Anderson, Palo Alto, California.

Polychromatic

DESIGN HINT
- A straight-cut black-and-white stripe binding can be a perfect finishing touch for a black-and-white quilt.

SPECTRUM FLIGHT

Julie Anderson has collected black-on-white and white-on-black prints for years. The block was a perfect match for alternating blocks. I suggested she try a black-gray-and-white art deco print in the large triangle propellers. This fabric really makes the quilt. The swirling print is perfect for her airplane theme. What an anniversary present for her pilot husband to hang in his office!

Rule #1: Color = polychromatic

Rule #2: Small propellers = black-on-white print or white-on-black print, alternating by block

Rule #3: Rings = spectrum of solids

Rule #4: Corners = opposite of propeller color by alternating block

Rule #5: Large propellers = art deco print

Rule #6: Centers = matches ring

Air Ship Propeller is our most complex block; with five templates and zones to think about. However, the design process remains the same. Focus on one zone at a time and collect fabrics for it. You'll probably want to start with the large and small propellers. One decision leads to the next. You won't be sewing the blocks until they're all composed, so you can fine-tune as you go along.

CHAPTER TWELVE

Putting It All Together

Chicago O'Hare International Airport.
Photo by author.

When I took up machine quilting, I just wanted to wake up the next day and be Harriet Hargrave. It didn't happen. While I never became a wonderful machine quilter like Harriet, I did grow and develop my own style. Now people tell me they wish they could machine quilt like me! We all have to pay our dues and put in the time. The same thing happens with color and design.

You can become a better quilter one day at a time. Sometimes the progress is slow; sometimes it's fast. If you work on trying the following, you can take control of what happens in your quilts:

Learn to see how design is used in every day life.

- Learn to really look for and see the color around you.

- Learn to see how design is used in every day life.

- Learn to buy and use new colors.

- Learn to look for and buy colorways.

- Learn to buy warm and cool versions of the same color so you can purposely mismatch.

- Learn to buy and use new fabric types.

- Learn to buy variations on a theme by amassing a special collection of fabric.

CHAPTER THIRTEEN

General Instructions and Helpful Hints

Make accurate templates by carefully tracing patterns provided onto plastic template material.

Cut fabric accurately.

- When using a one-way template, stack fabric for cutting so you see the right side of all layers. Do not fold the fabric for multiple cutting or you will end up with mirror-image pieces that will not work in the same quilt.

Fold

Folded fabric with one-way template = half of the pieces are wrong.

Stack layers, all right-side up = all pieces are correct.

- To cut curves around a template with a rotary cutter, trace around the template with a pencil or chalk, remove the template, and rotary cut on the line.

- It is okay to layer fabric for cutting, except for stripes, which may need to be fussy-cut one layer at a time.

- It is more interesting to use an odd (rather than even) number of elements from each fabric; such as 1, 3, or 5 pinwheels.

Compose entire quilt on your design wall—NO STITCHING YET.

- Take a Polaroid or digital photo of the finished composition for easy reference in case you get mixed up during the sewing process.

Devise a system to remove and stitch a limited number of blocks at once. (I stitch up to three blocks at a time, but sometimes one is enough.)

- Arrange individual blocks on "carrying boards." (Place sheets of fine sandpaper on 8½" x 11" pieces of cardboard. Secure around the edges with tape.) The sandpaper will hold the fabric during transport. They are light to carry and easy to stack. You may want to number them.

Carrying boards.

- Use a pin to mark the left-hand side, or top, of the block(s) as you take the pieces down.

Make sure you are stitching accurately so the blocks turn out a consistent size.

- Check to be sure you are stitching ¼" seams. The blocks I have selected are mostly simple; none is really difficult. However, you must be precise.

- To ensure accurate seams, use a ¼" presser foot on your machine. (Special feet can be purchased or the needle position can be moved to the right.) Check by stitching on 4-to-the-inch graph paper to make sure.

- Use the single-stitch throat plate on your machine, rather than the zigzag one, so the fabric will not be sucked down into the machine. (Do not try the single-stitch throat plate if you have moved your needle position.)

- Begin new lines of stitching by making a few stitches on an "on-and-off" (small scrap of fabric) and stitch to the edge. Continue stitching right onto the real seam. (It won't hurt your machine if a few stitches aren't actually anchored in fabric.)

- Continue stitching between block pieces in a chain fashion. In this way, there is a continuous line of stitching from edge to edge as each seam is stitched, and seams will be less likely to come undone. Chaining also keeps pieces in order when you are stitching multiple blocks at once.

- Use a seam ripper or large pin to guide the end of the seam if it wants to swerve as it feeds through the machine. (Triangles are most likely to do this.)

- Pin seams, if necessary, to keep the pieces lined up properly. When placing pins, put the head away from the edge of the fabric so it won't be in the way of the presser foot. The head will be to the left, which is opposite of the way you were taught to pin seams in dressmaking where you stitch larger seam allowances.

- Always pin each end, then the middle of the two pieces to be joined. If one piece seems to be slightly larger than the other, place it on the bottom, next to the feed dogs, to ease in the fullness.

- Carefully sew over the pins. (Eventually the needle will get a burr on the tip. Replace it when this happens.)

Stitch the block(s) according to individual quilt instructions. Finger-press each seam as you go.

- Return the block(s) to the design wall. Check placement by putting the "marking" straight pin in the correct position. Look at the surrounding blocks to make sure you are keeping the pattern. Consult the photo, if necessary.

- Press each block with an iron after all the blocks have been pieced for that row.

When all blocks have been pieced and pressed, join into rows. Press seams of Row 1 to the left, seams of Row 2 to the right, and so on.

- Join Row 1 to Row 2. Press the seams of the joined rows down toward the bottom of the quilt.

- Continue until all rows have been joined.

Finish the quilt.

- Layer, baste, and quilt.

- Bind using your preferred method.

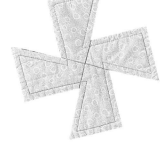

Sunshine and Windmills

Quilt is 8 units x 8 units and measures 48½" x 48½".

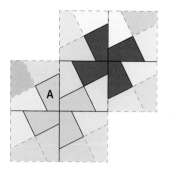

The visual design is created when four same-color identical pieces in adjoining units touch and form pinwheels. How you see it is not how you sew it. The 6" pieced unit is constructed from four different color pieces. Each is a part of a different pinwheel.

Sunshine and Windmills, 48½" x 48½". 1999. Karen Dugas, Pleasant Hill, CA. Quilted by New Pieces, Berkeley, California

MATERIALS

Fabric requirements are based on 42" fabric width.

Pinwheels

- ¼ yard each of 21–23 different fabrics OR 64 scraps at least 4½" x 16½"

Notes

- If you want the stripes to run lengthwise on the pinwheel, you will need extra fabric; at least 5" x 16½" for each pinwheel.
- Approximately half of the fabrics are in blue/blue-violet/violet and half in orange/yellow-orange/yellow.

Backing

53" x 53"

Binding

½ yard

Batting

53" x 53"

Template plastic

CUTTING

Pinwheels

(Use pattern A)

- Cut 4 pieces from each rectangle or 12 pieces from each ¼ yard (256 total).

Notes

- If you stack-cut the pieces, each layer of fabric must be right side up or some of the cut pieces will be backward.
- If you use a stripe, fussy-cut one layer at a time to make sure all 4 pinwheel pieces have the same line orientation (page 98).

Binding

- Cut 6 strips 2" x fabric width. Sew into one long strip.

QUILT TOP CONSTRUCTION

Use ¼" seam allowance. Refer to the General Instructions beginning on page 90.

1. Lay out all pieces on a design wall referring to the photograph and illustration.
2. Pick up individual units on carrying boards (see page 90).

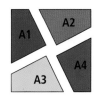

3. Stitch A1 to A2 and A3 to A4. Finger-press the seams in opposite directions so the seams will nest.

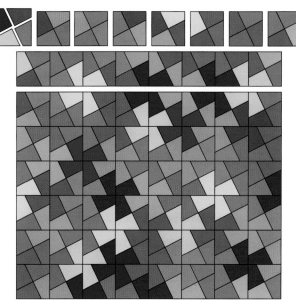

Quilt Construction

4. Stitch A1/A2 to A3/A4. Finger press.

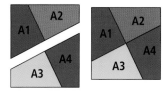

Pinwheel Unit

5. Repeat to complete 64 units. Press.
6. Sew the units into rows. Press.
7. Sew the rows together. Press.
8. Layer, baste, quilt, and bind.

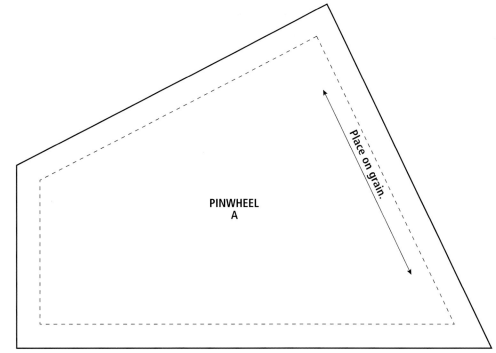

PINWHEEL
A

Place on grain.

Triad Double Stars

Quilt is 8 units x 10 units and
measures 48½" x 60½".

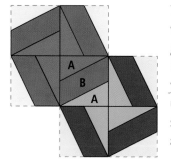

The visual design is created
when four same-color triangles touch and form stars.
How you see it is not how
you sew it. The 6" pieced
unit is constructed by
stitching two triangles to
a parallelogram.

Triad Double Stars, 48½" x 60½". 2002. Mary Mashuta. Quilted by Barbara Wilson, Citrus Heights, California.

MATERIALS

Fabric requirements are based on 42" fabric width.

Stars

- ¼ yard each of 5–7 different red-orange fabrics OR 20 scraps 8" x 8½" or 4" x 16"
- ¼ yard each of 5–7 different yellow-green fabrics OR 20 scraps 8" x 8½" or 4" x 16"

Note: For vertical stripes you will need twice as much fabric.

Background

- ⅛ yard each of 20 different blue-violet fabrics (You will get 4 background pieces from each ⅛ yard.) OR 20 scraps 3½" x 33"

Backing

53" x 65"

Binding

½ yard stripe fabric

Batting

53" x 65"

Template plastic

CUTTING

Stars

(Use pattern A. Mark right side.)

- Cut 4 triangles from each rectangle using template A OR cut 2 rectangles 3¾" x 7¼", then cut in half corner to corner as shown (4 triangles per star, 80 total of each color).

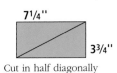

7¼"

3¾"

Cut in half diagonally

Cut two rectangles with the stripe going the same direction for each star.

Notes

- If you stack cut the pieces, each layer of fabric must be right side up or some of the cut pieces will be backward. (No folding for the same reason.) If cutting without a template, be careful to cut all rectangles from corner to corner at the angle shown.
- If you use stripes, make sure all four star pieces have the same line orientation. I prefer stripes to be parallel to the base of the triangle. Fussy-cut one layer at a time.

Background

(Use pattern B. Mark right side.)

- Cut 4 parallelograms from each of the 20 blue-violet fabrics (80 total).

Binding

- Cut 6 strips 2" x fabric width. Sew into one long strip.

QUILT TOP CONSTRUCTION

Use ¼" seam allowance. Refer to the General Instructions beginning on page 90.

1. Lay out all pieces on a design wall referring to the photograph and illustration.

2. Pick up individual units on carrying boards (see page 90). Mark the corner dots on the pieces.

Mark corner dots.

3. With B on top, stitch A to B matching the corner dots. The feed dogs will ease in any bias fullness. Finger-press the seam toward B.

Stitch A to B.

4. Stitch the second A triangle to B. Finger-press the seam toward B.

Star Unit

5. Repeat to complete 80 units. Press.
6. Sew the units into rows. Press.
7. Sew the rows together. Press.
8. Layer, baste, quilt, and bind.

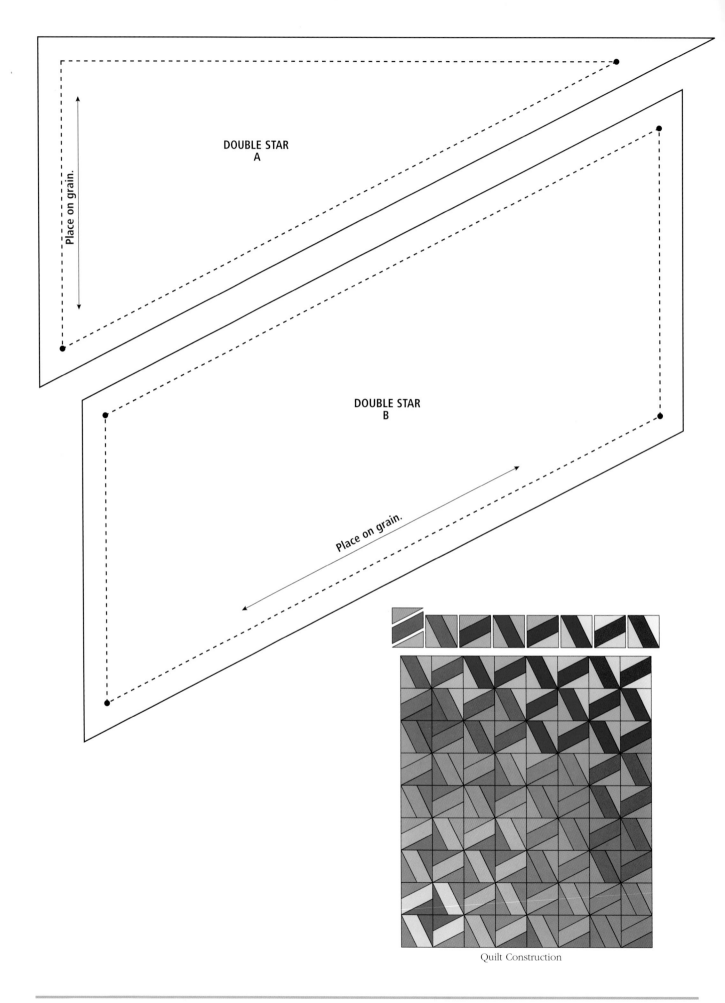

DOUBLE STAR
A

Place on grain.

DOUBLE STAR
B

Place on grain.

Quilt Construction

Raspberry Swirl

Quilt is 16 units x 18 units + a 2" border and measures 84½" x 94½".

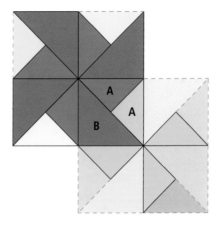

The visual design is created when four same-color triangles touch and form pinwheels. Four large triangles form a large pinwheel and four small triangles form a small pinwheel. How you see it is not how you sew it. The 5" pieced unit is constructed from one large triangle and two small triangles. Each is part of a different pinwheel. Half-blocks at the edge create a visual border.

Raspberry Swirl. 84½" x 94½". 2002. Becky Keck, Martinez, California. Quilted by New Pieces, Berkeley, California.

MATERIALS

Fabric requirements are based on 42" fabric width.

Large Pinwheels

● ¼ yard each of 28 different red-violet fabrics OR 56 scraps 6" x 12½" (4½" x 22" if cutting stripes)

Small Pinwheels

● ¼ yard each of 16 different yellow-orange fabrics OR 64 scraps 3½" x 16" (template) OR 64 scraps 6¼" x 6¼" (quick rotary cutting)

● ¼ yard each of 16 different blue-green fabrics OR 64 scraps 3½" x 16" (template) OR 64 scraps 6¼" x 6¼" (quick rotary cutting)

Border

2½ yards of raspberry dot fabric

Backing

89" x 99"

Binding

⅝ yard

Batting

89" x 99"

Template plastic

CUTTING

Small Pinwheels

(Use pattern A)

● Cut 4 triangles from each rectangle either using template A OR cut rectangles or ¼-yard pieces into two squares 6¼" x 6¼", then cut diagonally twice corner to corner (512 total).

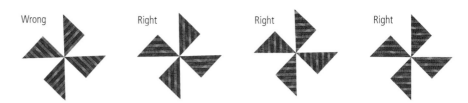

Wrong   Right   Right   Right

Triangles cut from squares won't twirl. Cut 4 triangles exactly alike.

Note: If you use stripes, make sure all four triangles have the same line orientation. Fussy-cut one layer at a time so they twirl.

Large Pinwheels

(Use pattern B)

● Cut 4 triangles from each red-violet rectangle or 8 triangles from each ¼-yard piece using template B OR cut into squares 5⅞" x 5⅞", then cut in half corner to corner (224 total).

Note: Do not try to quick cut stripe or plaid triangles from squares. You will end up with lines all going the same way and the pinwheel won't twirl.

Border

(Use patterns A and B)

● Cut 64 small triangles (A) from raspberry dot OR cut 16 squares 6¼" x 6¼", then cut diagonally twice corner to corner.

● Cut 64 large triangles (B) from raspberry dot OR cut 32 squares 5⅞" x 5⅞", then cut in half corner to corner.

● Cut 9 strips 2½" x fabric width from raspberry dot. Sew into one long strip. From this: Cut 2 strips 2½" x 90½" for the sides. Cut 2 strips 2½" x 80½" for the top and bottom.

Binding

● Cut 10 strips 2" x fabric width. Sew into one long strip.

QUILT TOP CONSTRUCTION

Use ¼" seam allowance.
Refer to the General Instructions beginning on page 90.

1. Lay out all pieces on a design wall referring to the photograph and illustration. Note where the raspberry dot triangles are placed to create the border.

2. Pick up individual blocks on carrying boards (see page 90).

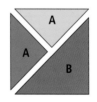

3. Stitch A to A. Finger-press the seam to one side.

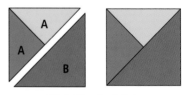

Triple Pinwheel Unit

4. Stitch A/A to B. Finger-press toward B.

5. Repeat to complete 288 units. Press.

6. Sew the units into rows. Press.

7. Sew the rows together. Press.

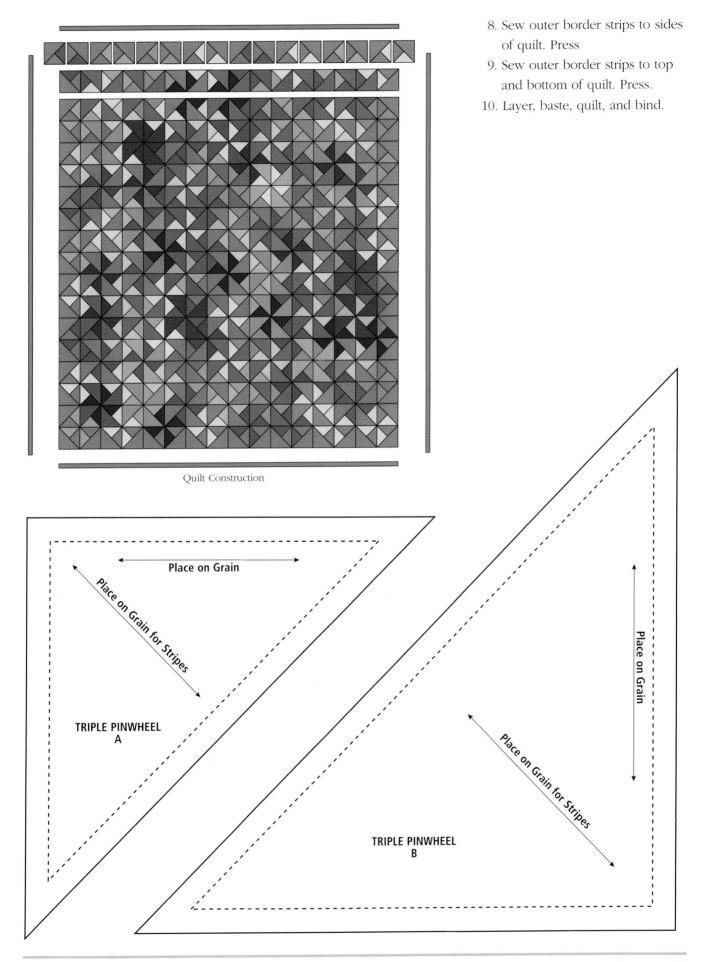

8. Sew outer border strips to sides of quilt. Press

9. Sew outer border strips to top and bottom of quilt. Press.

10. Layer, baste, quilt, and bind.

Quilt Construction

Place on Grain

Place on Grain for Stripes

TRIPLE PINWHEEL
A

Place on Grain

Place on Grain for Stripes

TRIPLE PINWHEEL
B

Dotty Arches

Quilt is 8 units x 8 units and
measures 50½" x 50½".

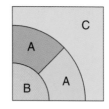

The 6¼" pieced unit is
constructed from two A
wedges, which are sewn
to a B quarter-circle and
a C corner.

Dotty Arches, 50½" x 50½". 2001. Karen Dugas, Pleasant Hill, California. Quilted by New Pieces, Berkeley, California.

MATERIALS

Fabric requirements are based on 42" fabric width.

Wedges

● ⅛ yard each of at least 13 different medium-dark to dark muted and neutral-colored fabrics OR 128 scraps 3½" x 4¾"

Quarter-Circles

● ⅛ yard each of at least 5 different light to medium muted and neutral-colored fabrics OR 64 scraps 3¼" x 3¼" (Use scraps 3¼" x 4½" from stripes or other directional prints.)

Outer Corners

● ¼ yard each of at least 8 different light to medium muted and neutral-colored fabrics OR 64 scraps 7" x 7"

Backing

55" x 55"

Binding

½ yard

Batting

55" x 55"

Template plastic

CUTTING

Wedges

(Use pattern A)

● Cut 128 wedges.

Quarter-Circles

(Use pattern B)

● Cut 64 quarter-circles.

Notes

• It is important to cut stripes or other directional prints with grain line in the diagonal middle of the quarter-circle. (Hold the template like a fan.)

• Mark the center of the curve (or crease the mid-point before pinning).

Outer Corners

(Use pattern C)

● Cut 64 outer corners.

Note: Mark the center of the curve (or crease the mid-point before pinning).

Binding

● Cut 6 strips 2" x fabric width. Sew into one long strip.

QUILT TOP CONSTRUCTION

Use ¼" seam allowance.
Refer to the General Instructions beginning on page 90.

1. Lay out all pieces on a design wall referring to the photograph and illustration.
2. Pick up individual units on carrying boards (page 90).

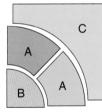

3. Stitch A to A. Finger-press in one direction. Carefully clip the seam allowance of the concave curve of A/A.

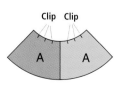

4. Place A/A on top of B, right sides together. Pin matching the center and corners. Stitch, leaving the pins in place. Remove the pins and finger-press toward B.

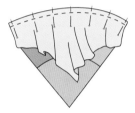

5. Place C on top of A/A, right sides together. Pin matching the center and corners. (Clipping optional.) Stitch, leaving the pins in place. Remove the pins and finger-press toward A/A.

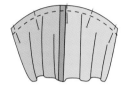

6. Repeat to make 64 units. Press.
7. Sew the units into rows. Press.
8. Sew the rows together. Press.
9. Layer, baste, quilt, and bind.

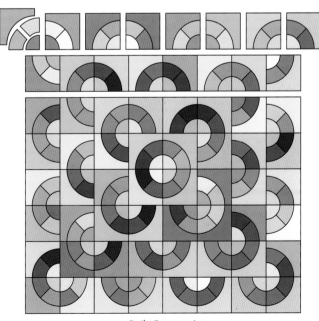

Quilt Construction

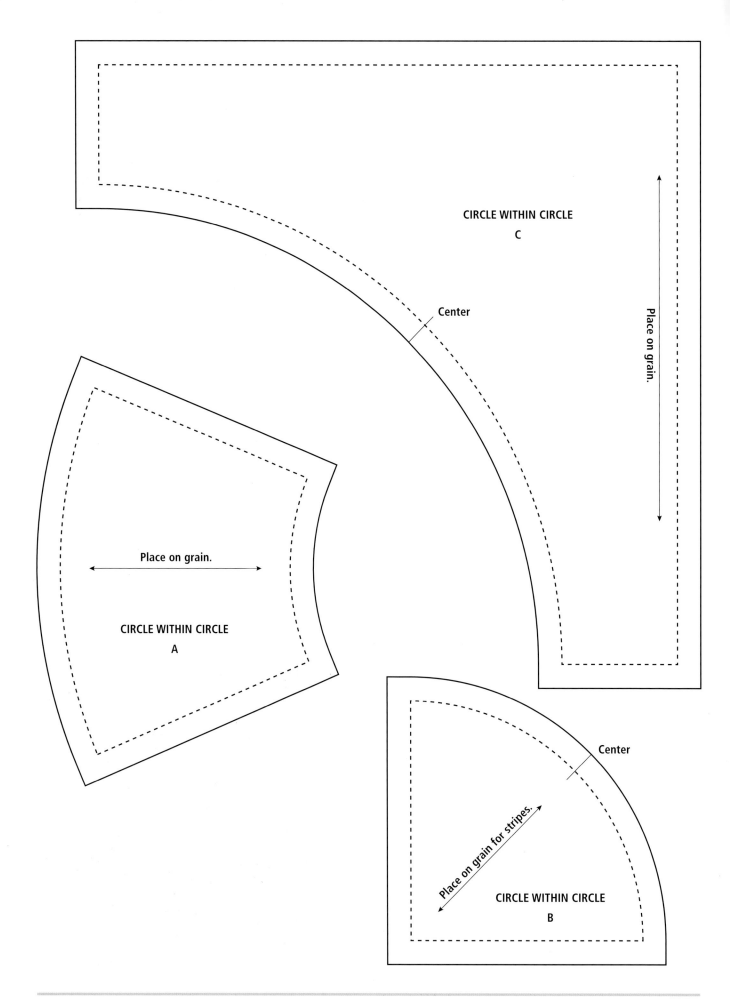

CIRCLE WITHIN CIRCLE
C

Place on grain.

Center

CIRCLE WITHIN CIRCLE
A

Place on grain.

Center

Place on grain for stripes.

CIRCLE WITHIN CIRCLE
B

A Few Days in Provence

Quilt is 9 blocks x 9 blocks and measures 63½" x 63½".

The visual design is created when same-fabric and similar-color pieces flow into each other, sometimes turning corners. The block is made up of two units which are made with two pieces, a polygon and a quarter-circle. Color flows are created by repeating fabrics or colors in diagonal adjoining blocks.

How you see it is not how you sew it, because the eye sees the color flows and not the individual blocks. The pieced unit is constructed when the polygon is sewn to the quarter-circle. Two units are then sewn together along the base of the polygons to form the 7" block.

A Few Days in Provence. 63½" x 63½". 1998. Mary Mashuta.

MATERIALS

Fabric requirements are based on 42" fabric width.

Try to collect as wide a range of stripes in your color palette as possible. Refer to What's Special About Stripes (page 19). Different colorways of the same stripe work well when you want to turn a corner.

You will need a total of 162 polygons, but multiples of each stripe are cut. I group from two to five same-fabric pieces in a flow of pattern and color. Another set of the same stripe could be placed elsewhere in the design.

Polygons

- ½ yard each of 10–12 assorted stripes OR 162 scraps 3½" x 11½" cut with the stripes perpendicular to long edge.

Quarter-Circles

- ⅛ yard each of 21 French Provençal prints, wispy solids, geometric prints, cloud prints, and/or assorted stripes OR 162 scraps 4½" x 6". Do not repeat polygon fabrics for the quarter-circles.

Backing

68" x 68"

Binding

½ yard stripe fabric

Batting

68" x 68"

Template plastic

CUTTING

Polygons

(Use pattern A)

- Cut 162 polygons.

Notes

- Cut stripes perpendicular to the base of the polygon. (Cut stripes so they look like the pickets in a picket fence.)
- Fussy-cut one layer at a time so stripes will not be accidentally cut off-grain and look crooked.(Don't let the pickets fall down.)
- Audition to see if you want to line up the center of the even stripes exactly alike so they can chevron when they turn a corner.

Quarter-Circles

(Use pattern B)

- Cut 162 quarter-circles.

Notes

- Stripes and geometric prints will look best when cut with the diagonal grain line on the template placed on a stripe so a radiating effect is produced. Think of a fan.
- If you use cloud fabrics, you will have to change position of template so the clouds always appear right side up to the viewer.

Binding

- Cut 7 strips 2" x fabric width. Sew into one long strip.

QUILT TOP CONSTRUCTION

Use ¼" seam allowance.
Refer to the General Instructions beginning on page 90.

1. Lay out all pieces on a design wall. Refer to the photograph and illustration.
2. Pick up the individual units on carrying boards (page 90). Mark center on each curve (or crease the mid-point before pinning).

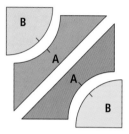

3. Clip the seam allowance of the concave curve of A. Place A on top of B, right sides together. Pin matching the center and corners. (You may want to add two additional pins.) Stitch, leaving the pins in place. Remove the pins and finger-press toward A.
4. Repeat Step 3 for the second half of the unit. Stitch the two units together along the long polygon edges. Finger-press.

Serpentine Curves
Block

5. Make 81 blocks. Press.
6. Sew the blocks into rows. Press.
7. Sew the rows together. Press.
8. Layer, baste, quilt, and bind.

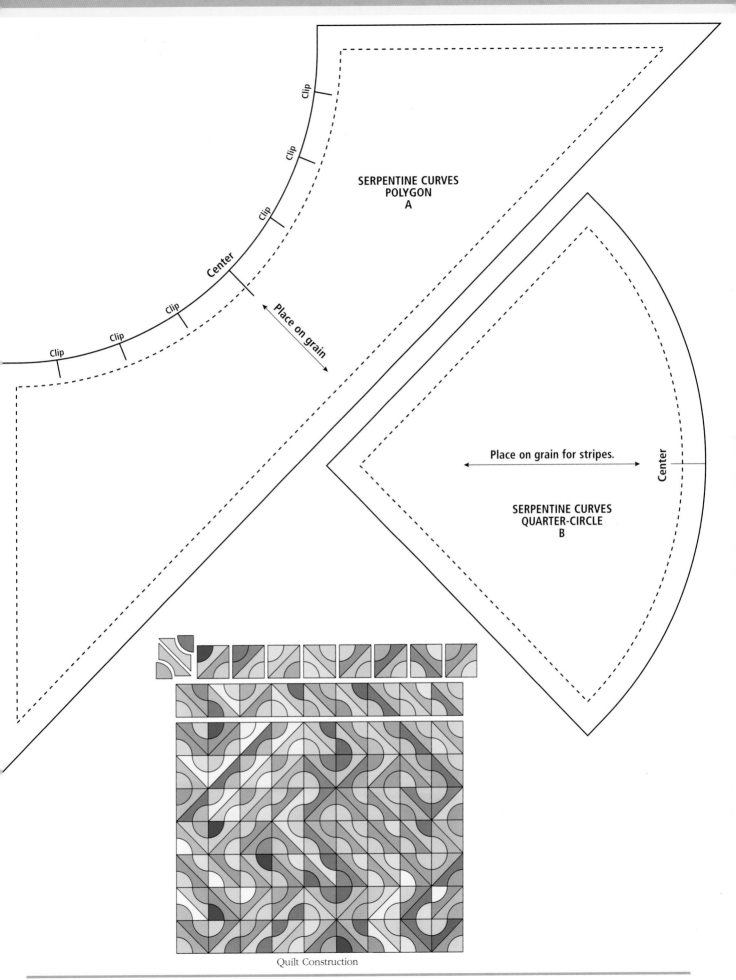

Clip

Clip

Clip

Center

Clip

Clip

Clip

Clip

SERPENTINE CURVES
POLYGON
A

Place on grain

Place on grain for stripes.

Center

SERPENTINE CURVES
QUARTER-CIRCLE
B

Quilt Construction

Paisley Propellers

Quilt is 4 blocks x 4 blocks + borders and
corners and measures 63½" x 63½".

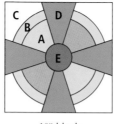

10" block

Air Ship Propeller is a block that
has five zones. The traditional
positive space consists of the
propellers, propeller rings, and
centers. The negative space is
created when four corners join with
the four large triangular pieces
between them. In this contemporary
version, the large triangular pieces
are cut from stripe fabric and
become additional propellers.

Paisley Propellers, 63½" x 63½". 2002. Mary Mashuta.

MATERIALS

Fabric requirements are based on 42" fabric width.

Small Propellers (A)
- ⅛ yard each of at least 6 paisley prints OR 64 scraps 3¼" x 4¼" (If cut 4 at a time, you need 16 rectangles 3¼" x 13½".)

Propeller Rings (B)
- ⅛ yard each of 4 different yellow fabrics OR 64 scraps 2" x 5"

Propeller Corners (C)
- ¼ yard each of 4 dot print fabrics

Stripe Propellers (D)
- ½ yard light stripe. (You will need additional fabric if you are using a wide stripe or one with an uneven repeat pattern.)
- ¾ yard dark stripe. (You will need additional fabric if you are using a wide stripe or one with an uneven repeat pattern.)

Circles (E) and Outer Corners
⅝ yard pink dot

Inner Border
⅝ yard paisley print

Inner Corners
4 yellow scraps 4" x 4"

Outer Border
1¼ yards of yellow floral

Stripe Corner Pieces
⅜ yard stripe

Backing
68" x 68"

Binding
½ yard pink stripe

Batting
68" x 68"

Template cardboard

CUTTING

Small Propellers
(Use pattern A)
- Cut 64 from paisley fabrics.

Propeller Rings
(Use pattern B)
- Cut 16 from each of the 4 yellow fabrics.

Propeller Corners
(Use pattern C)
- Cut 16 corners from each of 4 dot print fabrics.

Stripe Propellers
(Use pattern D)

Notes
- Stripes vary in width and pattern repeat so you may not get identical strips from your fabric. You will have to decide whether this makes any difference or not.
- Place template in same position on the stripe so the same stripe will run parallel to the base of the template.

FOR LIGHT STRIPES:
- Cut 6 strips 4½" x fabric length parallel to the selvage, then cut 4 propellers from each strip for a total of 24 propellers.

FOR DARK STRIPES:
- Cut eight 4½" strips parallel to the selvage, then cut 5 propellers from each strip for a total of 40 propellers.

Circles
(Use pattern E)
- Cut 16 circles from pink dot fabric.

Inner Border
- Cut 4 strips 4" x 40½" from paisley print fabric.

Inner Corners
- Cut 4 squares 4" x 4" from yellow fabric.

Outer Border
- Cut 4 strips 8½" x 40½" from yellow floral fabric.

Stripe Corner Pieces
- Cut 8 rectangles 4" x 8½" with stripe perpendicular to long edge.

Outer Corners
- Cut 4 squares 8½" x 8½" from pink dot fabric.

Binding
- Cut 7 strips 2" x fabric width. Sew into one long strip.

QUILT TOP CONSTRUCTION

Use ¼" seam allowance. Refer to the General Instructions beginning on page 90.

1. Place all pieces on a design wall referring to the photograph or illustration.
2. Pick up the individual blocks on carrying boards (page 90). Mark centers of the curves of pieces A, B, and C.

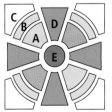

Air Ship Propeller Block

3. Place B on top of A, with right sides together. Pin the concave edge of B to the convex edge of A, matching centers and corners. Add two more pins to keep the fabric edges together. Stitch, leaving the pins in place. Remove the pins and finger-press toward A.

4. Place C on top of B, with right sides together. Pin the concave edge of C to the remaining edge of B by matching the centers and corners. Add two pins to keep the two fabric edges together. Stitch, leaving the pins in place. Finger-press toward B.

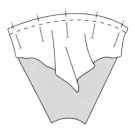

5. Stitch and A/B/C unit to the left side of each D piece, being careful that the propeller rings will align to form a circle when the units are sewn together. Finger-press seams toward D. Join the 4 units. Press.
6. Make 16 blocks.
7. Remove the seam allowance of circle E and make a card-board template.

8. With needle and thread, make a running stitch ⅛" from the edge of the fabric circle. Insert the template and gather up the fabric around the template's edge. Knot the thread to secure. Turn over and press. Remove the template. Make 16 circles.

9. Appliqué the circle in place with invisible appliqué stitches. You may want to add additional buttonhole or blanket stitching by machine or by hand using perle cotton.

10. Sew the blocks into rows. Press.
11. Sew the rows together. Press.
12. Stitch inner borders to the sides of the quilt top. Press toward the borders.
13. Stitch a yellow inner corner to each end of the remaining inner borders. Stitch to the top and bottom of the quilt top. Press toward the borders.
14. Stitch a stripe corner rectangle to each end of the 2 outer borders. Stitch to the sides of the quilt top. Press toward the outer borders.
15. Stitch a stripe corner rectangle and an outer corner to each end of the remaining outer borders. Stitch to the top and bottom of the quilt top. Press toward the outer borders.
16. Layer, baste, quilt, and bind.

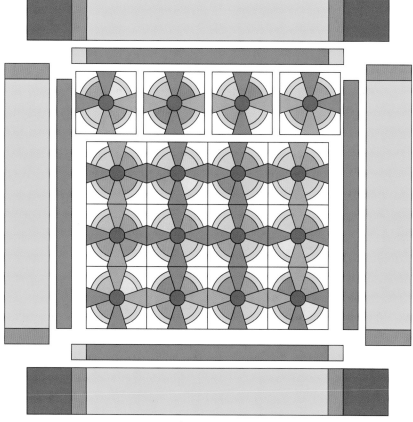

Quilt Construction

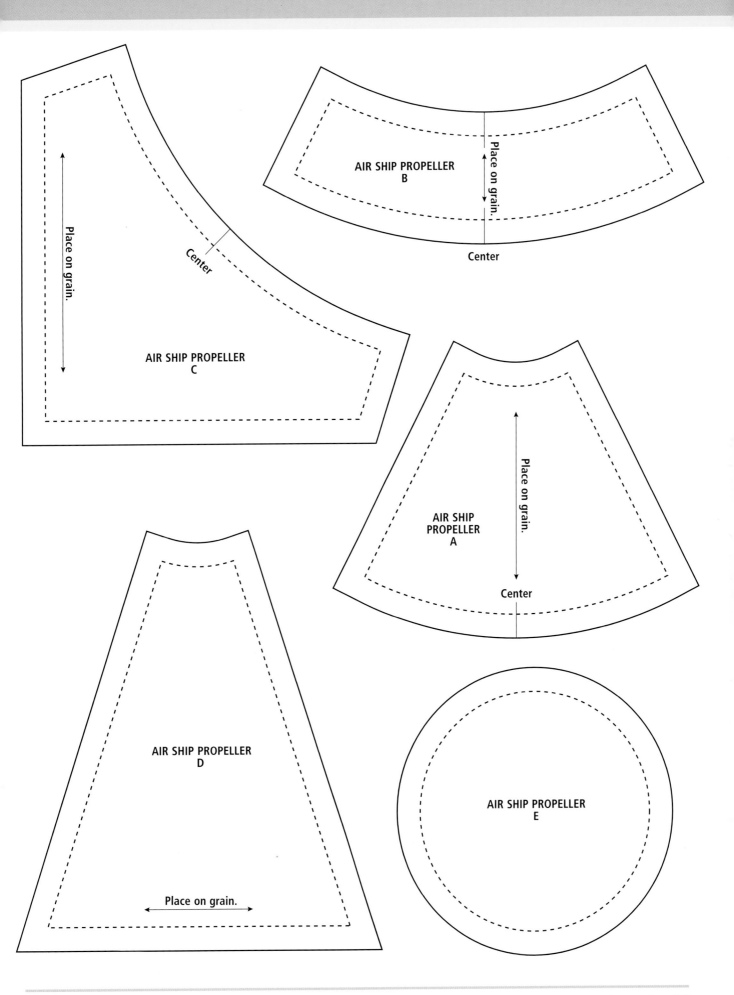

AIR SHIP PROPELLER
B

Place on grain.

Center

Place on grain.

Center

AIR SHIP PROPELLER
C

AIR SHIP
PROPELLER
A

Place on grain.

Center

AIR SHIP PROPELLER
D

Place on grain.

AIR SHIP PROPELLER
E

About the Author

Mary has loved working with fabric since she fashioned her first doll clothes as a child. She purchased one of the few quilt books available in the sixties and immediately fell in love with quilting. Many years and quilts later, she still loves fabric and quilts.

Mary firmly believes that you can never own too much fabric. Her goal is to experience the joy of using as much of it as possible. She is always in search of simple blocks that will allow her to "fast forward" to color and fabric selection and circumvent difficult construction.

Mary has two degrees in home economics. She is a professionally trained teacher and has taught quiltmaking internationally. This is her fifth book with C&T Publishing. She lives in Berkeley, California with her sister, fellow quilter Roberta Horton.

Index

15 Two-Block Quilts: Unlock the Secrets of Secondary Patterns, Claudia Olson

250 Continuous-Line Quilting Designs for Hand, Machine & Long-Arm Quilters, Laura Lee Fritz

250 More Continuous-Line Quilting Designs for Hand, Machine & Long-Arm Quilters, Laura Lee Fritz

All About Quilting from A to Z, From the Editors and Contributors of *Quilter's Newsletter Magazine* and *Quiltmaker* magazine

Along the Garden Path: More Quilters and Their Gardens, Jean & Valori Wells

America from the Heart: Quilters Remember September 11, 2001, Karey Bresenhan

An Amish Adventure, 2nd Edition: A Workbook for Color in Quilts, Roberta Horton

Art of Classic Quiltmaking, The, Harriet Hargrave & Sharyn Craig

Art of Machine Piecing, The: How to Achieve Quality Workmanship Through a Colorful Journey, Sally Collins

Beautifully Quilted with Alex Anderson: • How to Choose or Create the Best Designs for Your Quilt • 6 Timeless Projects • Full-Size Patterns, Ready to Use, Alex Anderson

Bouquet of Quilts, A: Garden-Inspired Projects for the Home, edited by Jennifer Rounds & Cyndy Lyle Rymer

Civil War Women: Their Quilts, Their Roles & Activities for Re-Enactors, Barbara Brackman

Color from the Heart: Seven Great Ways to Make Quilts with Colors You Love, Gai Perry

Come Listen to My Quilts: •Playful Projects •Mix & Match Designs, Kristina Becker

Contemporary Classics in Plaids & Stripes: 9 Projects from Piece 'O Cake Designs, Linda Jenkins & Becky Goldsmith

Cotton Candy Quilts: Using Feed Sacks, Vintage, and Reproduction Fabrics, Mary Mashuta

Cozy Cabin Quilts from Thimbleberries: 20 Projects for Any Home, Lynette Jensen

Create Your Own Quilt Labels!, Kim Churbuck

Cut-Loose Quilts: Stack, Slice, Switch, and Sew, Jan Mullen

Dresden Flower Garden: A New Twist on Two Quilt Classics, Blanche Young

Elm Creek Quilts: Quilt Projects Inspired by the Elm Creek Quilts Novels, Jennifer Chiaverini & Nancy Odom

Everything Flowers: Quilts from the Garden, Jean & Valori Wells

Fantastic Fabric Folding: Innovative Quilting Projects, Rebecca Wat

Four Seasons in Flannel: 23 Projects—Quilts & More, Jean Wells & Lawry Thorn

From Fiber to Fabric: The Essential Guide to Quiltmaking Textiles, Harriet Hargrave

Garden-Inspired Quilts: Design Journals for 12 Quilt Projects, Jean & Valori Wells

Hand Quilting with Alex Anderson: Six Projects for First-Time Hand Quilters, Alex Anderson

Heirloom Machine Quilting, Third Edition: Comprehensive Guide to Hand-Quilting Effects Using Your Sewing Machine, Harriet Hargrave

Hidden Block Quilts: • Discover New Blocks Inside Traditional Favorites • 13 Quilt Settings • Instructions for 76 Blocks, Lerlene Nevaril

Impressionist Palette: Quilt Color & Design, Gai Perry

Impressionist Quilts, Gai Perry

Laurel Burch Quilts: Kindred Creatures, Laurel Burch

Lone Star Quilts and Beyond: Step-by-Step Projects and Inspiration, Jan Krentz

Magical Four-Patch and Nine-Patch Quilts, Yvonne Porcella

Make Any Block Any Size: Easy Drawing Method, Unlimited Pattern Possibilities, Sensational Quilt Designs, Joen Wolfrom

Measure the Possibilities with Omnigrid®, Nancy Johnson-Srebro

Paper Piecing with Alex Anderson: •Tips •Techniques •6 Projects, Alex Anderson

Patchwork Persuasion: Fascinating Quilts from Traditional Designs, Joen Wolfrom

Patchwork Quilts Made Easy—Revised, 2nd Edition: 33 Quilt Favorites, Old & New, Jean Wells

Perfect Union of Patchwork & Appliqué, A, Darlene A. Christopherson

Pieced Flowers, Ruth B. McDowell

Pieced Vegetables, Ruth B. McDowell

Piecing: Expanding the Basics, Ruth B. McDowell

Q is for Quilt, Diana McClun & Laura Nownes

Quick Quilts for the Holidays: 11 Projects to Stamp, Stencil, and Sew, Trice Boerens

Quilting Back to Front: Fun & Easy No-Mark Techniques, Larraine Scouler

Quilting with Carol Armstrong: • 30 Quilting Patterns • Appliqué Designs • 16 Projects, Carol Armstrong

Quilting with the Muppets: 15 Fun and Creative Projects, The Jim Henson Company in association with the Sesame Workshop

Quilts for Guys: 15 Fun Projects For Your Favorite Fella, edited by Cyndy Lyle Rymer

Quilts from the Civil War: Nine Projects, Historic Notes, Diary Entries, Barbara Brackman

Quilts, Quilts, and More Quilts!, Diana McClun & Laura Nownes

Ultimate Guide to Longarm Quilting, The: • How to Use Any Longarm Machine • Techniques, Patterns & Pantographs • Starting a Business • Hiring a Longarm Machine Quilter, Linda Taylor

Radiant New York Beauties: 14 Paper-Pieced Quilt Projects, Valori Wells

Rotary Cutting with Alex Anderson: Tips, Techniques, and Projects, Alex Anderson

Rx for Quilters: Stitcher-Friendly Advice for Every Body, Susan Delaney-Mech

Say It with Quilts, Diana McClun & Laura Nownes

Scrap Quilts: The Art of Making Do, Roberta Horton

Setting Solutions, Sharyn Craig

Sew Much Fun: 14 Projects to Stitch & Embroider, Oklahoma Embroidery Supply & Design

Shadow Quilts, Patricia Magaret & Donna Slusser

Shadow Redwork™ with Alex Anderson: 24 Designs to Mix and Match, Alex Anderson

Shoreline Quilts: 15 Glorious Get-Away Projects, compiled by Cyndy Rymer

Show Me How to Machine Quilt: A Fun, No-Mark Approach, Kathy Sandbach

Simple Fabric Folding for Christmas: 14 Festive Quilts & Projects, Liz Aneloski

Simply Stars: Quilts That Sparkle, Alex Anderson

Skydyes: A Visual Guide to Fabric Painting, Mickey Lawler

Slice of Christmas from Piece O' Cake Designs, A, Linda Jenkins & Becky Goldsmith

Smashing Sets: Exciting Ways to Arrange Quilt Blocks, Margaret J. Miller

Start Quilting with Alex Anderson, 2nd Edition: Six Projects for First-Time Quilters, Alex Anderson

Stitch 'n Flip Quilts: 14 Fantastic Projects, Valori Wells

Stripes In Quilts, Mary Mashuta

Thimbleberries Housewarming, A: 22 Projects for Quilters, Lynette Jensen

Tradition with a Twist: Variations on Your Favorite Quilts, Blanche Young & Dalene Young-Stone

Travels with Peaky and Spike: Doreen Speckmann's Quilting Adventures, Doreen Speckmann

Wine Country Quilts: A Bounty of Flavorful Projects for Any Palette, Cyndy Lyle Rymer & Jennifer Rounds

Workshop with Velda Newman, A: Adding Dimension to Your Quilts, Velda E. Newman

For more information, ask for a free catalog:
C&T Publishing, Inc.
P.O. Box 1456
Lafayette, CA 94549
(800) 284-1114
Email: ctinfo@ctpub.com
Website: www.ctpub.com

For quilting supplies:
Cotton Patch Mail Order
3405 Hall Lane, Dept.CTB
Lafayette, CA 94549
(800) 835-4418
(925) 283-7883
Email:quiltusa@yahoo.com
Website: www.quiltusa.com

Note: Fabrics used in the quilts shown may not be currently available since fabric manufacturers keep most fabrics in print for only a short time.